Improve Your Marketing and Grow Your Business

Published by
Lotus Press

Improve Your Marketing and Grow Your Business

Keshu Patnaik

LOTUS PRESS

4263/3, Ansari Road,
Darya Ganj, New Delhi-110002

Lotus Press
4263/3, Ansari Road, Darya Ganj, New Delhi- 110002
Ph.: 32903912, 23280047 • E-mail : lotus_press@sify.com
www.lotuspress.co.in

Improve Your Marketing and Grow Your Business

ISBN: 81-8382-165-0
Reprint: 2010

Published by : **Lotus Press,** New Delhi
Printed at : DD Offset Printing Press, Noida

PREFACE

Business endeavours and activities today inevitably depend upon the machinations of marketing, adhering to the business ethic of acquiring, retaining and satisfying customers. With stiff competition being the norm of the business market. The market players constantly battle to out do each other, and the most effective weapon in the armoury of the modern-day entrepreneur is marketing. Marketing techniques not only expand the scope of business, but also add value to a product, and by extension, the brand or enterprise it is associated with. The ramifications of marketing are numerous and immensely useful in their multi-faceted form; as such, it counts as amongst the most valuable assets a corporation can utilise to broaden its base. Marketing too, however, needs constant changes and improvements in the way it is employed, much as the ever changing market itself where it works. Entrepreneurs then, have to recognise the need for updating their modes of product or service endorsement, and acknowledge its credit.

This book, written as a business help manual, seeks to bring forth both budding and established entrepreneurs the essentials of the art of marketing, as well as the constant evolution which is an integral part of it. Not only does the book equip readers with the fundamentals of business marketing, it also brings to their attention contemporary challenges, trends and developments in the field. In addition, it also brings to attention a general overview of the field which concentrates on its thirst for evermore improvement, and how this marketing facet can be tapped for business growth.

It is hoped that the book's insight on marketing skills serves useful for the readers.

Editor

CONTENTS

1

SETTING AND ACHIEVING BUSINESS GOALS

Your goals must generate excitement when you ponder their accomplishment. You must believe there is something in it for you to accomplish them. Sometimes, especially at work, if you perceive the end reward is worth the work, you will take on challenges in support of the organisation's goals. These goals might not be as close to your heart as your personal goals, but you work to achieve them for the good of the organisation and your success there.

TIPS TO SETTING SUCCESS AND PROGRESS

Here are three more tips that will help you experience awesome success in accomplishing your goals and living your resolutions.

Base Your Goals Firmly in Your Values

Hyrum Smith, the founder of Franklin Quest, later Franklin-Covey, Inc., developed a model for goal setting. Smith's "Success Triangle" puts governing values at the base of the goal setting process. Smith recommends that every goal is linked specifically to a governing value. For example, if diversity in the workforce is a value espoused by your organisation, then at least one goal must further diversity. Every goal should be linked to a governing value.

Short-term, mid-term and long-term goals are then established based upon the solid foundation of your values. If the goal you set is congruent with and allows you to live your most important values, you are more likely to accomplish the goal.

According to Gene Donohue set goals in all aspects of your life, to maintain your life balance.

The balance also helps you accomplish goals as each aspect of your life is represented in your goals. You are less likely to experience warring priorities if every aspect of your life has a value-based goal. He suggests goals in these arenas:

— Family and Home

— Financial and Career

— Spiritual and Ethical

— Physical and Health

— Social and Cultural

— Mental and Educational

Believe You Can Accomplish the Goal

Each of us has a little voice in our head. It is the voice of our sub-conscious, judging self. On a daily basis, we engage in self-talk; we comment on each situation we encounter. We discuss events and plans in our minds. Our commentary is both positive and negative. Positive thoughts and planning support the accomplishment of our goals. Negative thoughts and comments undermine our self-esteem and self-confidence, and negatively impact our ability to accomplish our goals.

Listen to your voice. You can change its tone by believing in yourself and in your ability to accomplish your goals and resolutions. Use this unconscious critic to positively support your goal setting success.

If you are a manager, one of your more important tasks is to support the development of positive self-esteem by your staff members. Your positive outlook and belief in their ability to accomplish great goals fosters their increased self-esteem and self-confidence. This, in turn, magnifies their ability to accomplish more and contribute more to your business.

Goals to Measurable Outcomes

Traditionally, goals were established around measurable outcomes. Don't tie yourself to setting only measurable goals, however; you may find yourself concentrating on the trivial, because it is measurable, rather than on your most important outcomes. Sometimes the most important goals, the non-urgent, critical goals, are hard to measure.

"Explore alternatives for a business in the World Wide Web," is tough to measure, whereas the steps, once you make a decision, are easy to measure. "Learn about new options and thinking around performance management," is tough to measure in any significant way. The next step, "design a new appraisal system," is easier to define and measure.

As you move up the management ranks, you may find more of your goals are harder to measure. The key measurable aspects of your job will likely be the results produced by your reporting staff. With goals that are hard to measure, start with a picture in your mind, that you commit to paper, that describes the outcome you are seeking. Make the picture as vivid as you can.

TIPS TO FUEL GOAL SETTING SUCCESS

Here are six more tips that will help you experience awesome success in accomplishing your goals and living your resolutions.

Write Your Goals

Writing out your goal is your commitment to achieving the goal. Writing a goal is a powerful statement in comparison with half-formulated thoughts in the back of your mind. It is the conscious promise to yourself to pay attention to the accomplishment of the goal. Writing out potential action plans and due dates makes the goal even more powerful.

Share your Goals with People who are Important to you

If you are certain your significant others will support the accomplishment of your goals, share them. Your manager is likely to support your goal accomplishment as your success is her success. Honestly assess the ability of family members, peers and friends to provide support. In close relationships, many different feelings, experiences and historical events are at play. If you don't believe you will have whole-hearted support, keep the goals to yourself.

Check Goal Setting and Achievement Progress Regularly

One of the weaknesses of any annual appraisal system is the lack of frequency with which progress and success are measured and tracked. You are most likely to accomplish the goals you set if you review them daily as part of your normal planning process.

Whether you use a paper planner or a personal computer, you can enter your goals, and schedule daily and weekly actions that support their accomplishment. The discipline of the daily review is a powerful goal accomplishment tool.

Take Action to Identify and Eliminate Obstacles to Goal Setting Success

Simply tracking your goals daily is not enough. If you're unhappy with your progress, you need to assess what is keeping you from accomplishing the goals. Ask yourself questions such as, "Is this goal really important?"

"Are there specific obstacles you are experiencing which are interfering with your ability to accomplish the goal?"

If you are not making progress on a particular goal, attempt to do a root cause analysis to determine why. In this era of the personal computer and cell phones, picture your goals automatically forwarding for 365 days. Talk about a daily reminder about failure!

Reward Yourself and Celebrate Goal Accomplishment

Even the accomplishment of a minor goal is cause for celebration. Don't depress yourself with thoughts about all you still have to do. Celebrate what you have done. Then move on to the next milestone.

Goals and New Year Resolutions Change

Periodically look at the goals you have set for this year. Are the goals still the right goals? Give yourself permission to change your goals and resolutions based on changing circumstances.

Don't spend an entire year failing to achieve a particular goal. Your time is better spent on achievement than on beating yourself up for lack of progress. Maybe you made the goal too big; maybe you set too many goals. Do an honest assessment; change what needs to change periodically, and move on.

Paying attention to the following guidelines can make all the difference in your year. Will this year be a year of triumph for you, a year of awesome success? Whatever your goals and resolutions, these tips can help power your success.

STEPS TO ACCOMPLISH YOUR GOALS AND RESOLUTIONS

Don't let your goals and resolutions fall by the wayside. Chances are that to achieve your dreams and live a life you love, those goals and resolutions are crucial. Goal setting and goal achievement are easier if you follow these six steps for effective and successful goal setting and resolution accomplishment.

Step 1: *You need to deeply desire the goal or resolution.* Napoleon Hill, in his landmark book, *Think and Grow Rich,* had it right. "The starting point of all achievement is desire. Keep this constantly in mind. Weak desires bring weak results, just as a small amount of fire makes a small amount of heat." So, your first step in goal setting and achieving your dreams is that you've got to really, really want to achieve the goal.

Step 2: *Visualise yourself achieving the goal.* Lee Iacocca said, "The greatest discovery of my generation is that human beings can alter their lives by altering their attitudes of mind." What will your achievement feel like? How will your life unfold differently as a result? If the goal is a thing, some gurus of goal setting recommend that you keep a picture of the item where you see and are reminded of it every day.

If you can't picture yourself achieving the goal, chances are – you won't.

Step 3: *Make a plan for the path you need to follow to accomplish the goal.* Create action steps to follow. Identify a critical path. The critical path defines the key accomplishments along the way, the most important steps that must happen for the goal to become a reality. Stephen Covey said, "All things are created twice. There's a mental or first creation, and a physical or second creation of all things. You have to make sure that the blueprint, the first creation, is really what you want, that you've thought everything through. Then you put it into bricks and mortar. Each day you go to the construction shed and pull out the blueprint to get marching orders for the day. You begin with the end in mind." He's right.

Step 4: *Commit to achieving the goal by writing down the goal.* Lee Iacocca said, "The discipline of writing something down is the first step toward making it happen." I agree completely. Write down the plan, the action steps and the critical path. Somehow, writing down the goal, the plan and a timeline sets events in motion that may not have happened otherwise. In my own life, it is as if I am making a deeper commitment to goal accomplishment. I can't fool myself later. The written objective really was the goal.

Step 5: *Establish times for checking your progress in your calendar system, whatever it is:* a day planner, a P.C., a cell phone or a hand written list. If you're not making progress or feel stymied, don't let your optimism keep you from accomplishing your goals. No matter how positively you are thinking, you need to assess your lack of progress. Adopt a pessimist's viewpoint; something will and probably is, going to go wrong. Take a look at all of the factors that are keeping you from accomplishing your goal and develop a plan to overcome them. Add these plan steps to your calendar system as part of your goal achievement plan.

Step 6: *Review your overall progress regularly.* Make sure you are making progress. If you are not making progress, hire a advisor, tap into the support of loved ones, analyse why the goal is not being met. Don't allow the goal to just fade away. Figure out what you need to do to accomplish it. Check the prior five steps starting with an assessment of how deeply you actually want to achieve the goal.

This six step goal setting and achieving system seems simple, but it is the most powerful system you will ever find for achieving your goals and living your resolutions. You just need to do it.

FAILURE OF GOAL SETTING

Beware the Misuse of Goal Setting

Why don't most people set and achieve personal goals, career goals and business goals? Goal setting is a positive, powerful practice when it ignites enthusiasm and provides clear direction.

When practiced poorly, however, goal setting also has a serious downside which can undermine your success. Poor goal setting makes people cynical, wastes their time and fosters confusion about where to concentrate actions and energy. How does such a potentially successful practice as goal setting, go wrong, so often?

Avoid these five misuses of a potentially positive, powerful practice: goal setting for personal goals, career goals and business goals.

Intimidation

Organisations often fail to achieve goals and strategic planning targets that are set top down, by executives who lack crucial information and are out of touch with staff challenges. The goals are unrealistic and they fail to consider organisation resources and capabilities. Staff members don't believe that the rewards they will receive for goal accomplishment will equal the energy they invest to achieve them. Frequently, managers are intimidated when they fear job loss for failure.

A former Siebel Systems executive says, "My favourite goal setting story of all time was how Siebel set sales goals for its District Managers: everyone's quota was $3.5 million. There, no more thought needed to go into it, no discussion - just do it or you're fired! So the District Manager calling on Citibank had the same quota as the District Manager calling on the States of Louisiana, Mississippi and Alabama. Guess which guy got fired?

"I also remember how I used to spend the last day of every sales quarter at Siebel performing unnatural acts to close business and save my job. At the end of the year, I had to work until 10:00 p.m. on the last day of the sales quarter (while we had company over at home) to get one last deal closed. This deal saved my job. I was one of two state and local district managers that avoided the axe two weeks later."

Goals Intended to Impress, Not Guide Efforts

William Hamilton says, "During the roaring, crazy days of the dot.com nineties, using goals to impress was common place, although organisations also utilised this technique long before the Internet arrived. In this process, management creates goals based on the desire to impress or mislead outside groups."

According to Hamilton, this process is, "also used to avoid serious analysis of the company and the marketplace. At the end of the time period, these goals can then be used by senior management to pass the buck and the blame for the failure to meet the goals.

"To internal staff members, who were often unconvinced and unmoved by the unrealistic, 'show goals,' senior management's actions produced serious morale and competency-questioning issues. To staff members who bought into the euphoria, failure to achieve the goals was a deadly downward spiral."

We Had to Destroy the Village

In an effort to meet the current period's goals, the long-term viability of the organisation is put at risk. Hamilton gives these examples of negative actions people take to meet unrealistic goals. "They:

- Focus development efforts on the next sale.
- Offer deep discounts on products to move future sales into the current period.
- Push expenses into the future, rather than accounting for them when incurred.
- Use expensive promotions that actually generate less in sales than they cost.
- Fail to carefully develop long-term strategic efforts, when 'strategic' means the payoff is not within the next goal time period."

A former IBM manager illustrates this point with this story.

"One ridiculous process was the way IBM used to set sales quotas. In the later years there, when the company was showing very slow growth, you could count on a 25-30 percent increase in quota. It didn't matter that most IT (Information Technology) budgets were stagnant, so the quota process was demoralising in a big way. The way to make dollars there, was to find a job where they weren't sure how to set the quota - some kind of new area - and clean up and move on. Some people specialised in this sort of behaviour."

Goal Setting Becomes About the Plan, Not the Execution

Hamilton says a potential serious downside occurs when "the ratio of energy, time and creativity that goes into creating the goal outstrips (and comes out of the hide) of actually managing the product."

In one small manufacturing company, a management group decided to use gantt charts to track goal accomplishment. After starting with a huge investment of time in making the charts for all of their goals, the management group soon abandoned the charting. When questioned later, they affirmed that the charting was taking too much of the time they needed to accomplish the goals. But, they had awesome charts while they were keeping them up.

Too Many Goals Make Nothing a Priority

People with too many goals experience with these issues.

— They never feel as if they accomplish a complete task.

— It is difficult to tie their goal accomplishment to a reward and recognition system that recognises their accomplishments.

— They don't know what is most important to accomplish next.

— They fall prey to the "check it off the list" syndrome in which they check tasks off their list before the actions have been integrated by the organisation.

Goal setting is a positive, powerful, business practice when it tells your staff where you are going. Effective goal setting also demonstrates what success will look like during the journey and upon arrival. When practiced poorly, however, goal setting can negatively impact your organisation in all the ways described, and more.

2

HOW TO DEVELOP MARKETING CAPABILITY

This capability has two basic building blocks: innovation and delivering that innovation to customers via branded solutions and experiences.

INNOVATION

Innovation should be the primary engine of growth. Two of the most powerful words in the marketing lexicon are "different" and "better." Those are customer-centric words. The customer is searching for solutions that are different and better. The companies that deliver on the needs for "different and better" are the ones with loyal customers and consistent top-line revenue growth.

How can you drive innovation? Where does it come from? Our contention is that it is both engendered and delivered by the marketing process. Marketing bestrides the field of innovation like a colossus. The first footprint is the *input* to the innovation process, which we call insights. The second footprint is the *output* of the innovation process, which is the brand experience.

Marketing should accurately tap consumer attitudes to provide the right goods and services. Then it can use scientific practices to influence consumer attitudes to change behaviour. The behaviour we seek to affect is the economic one of purchasing, loyalty, and increasing share of requirements. That can come only as a result of changing attitudes. This insight is critical, because it sheds light on the motivations that drive behaviour, and therefore on what we must do to change behaviour.

Insights build and sustain winning brands. They create advantage across the entire brand-building continuum, from the moment of truth contained in the core insight, to the moment of truth across the buyer's desk, to the in-use moment of truth when the customer experiences the product or service.

Moments of Truth

Every marketing team can win an increased share of the customer's heart by developing insights that allow the brand to own the "moment of truth." The three moments of truth are as follows:

1. *The core of your brand promise:* For Nike that seminal moment of truth is not about shoes; it's about "self-realisation through exercise." It's about Nike owning that feeling you get not from winning a race but from doing your best. To its millions of adherents, the Nike swoosh is a talismanic symbol that "I care about doing my very best."
2. *Just before the purchase, when the buyer is considering an array of choices:* This is the moment of truth at the shelf, where the customer passes judgement on the array of benefits, both real and emotional, you are offering her. For virtually all consumer packaged-goods brands, this has been the most neglected consumer touch point.
3. The product in-use and the combination of "brand touches" during that usage experience reinforce the

customer's loyalty to the brand. Apple's iPod in-use moment of truth combines the ease of downloading (and paying with your credit card!), the simplicity of using the iPod's software functions and interface, and the sensuousness of the design. No matter what your product or service, no matter whether your buyer is a 12-year-old girl using her iPod or a power shovel operator using your equipment, you must deliver an in-use moment of truth experience that is defined by the user.

Insights Generation

Insights generation is a core competency of the innovative company. That's why you should build a process and develop a best-practices organisational construct and a range of tools to turn your company into an insights-hungry, insights-discovery machine.

Process means transforming an input into an output that's of use to the customer. In our case, we've defined the output of the insights process as innovation and the brand experience. But knowledge is not insight. We can know something without understanding its implications. Insights generation is the establishment of a shared understanding of what drives customer behaviour. This includes sufficient utility for us to reinforce that behaviour (if it is favourable to us), to expand that behaviour to get the customer to buy more, or to change that behaviour by getting the customer to switch from the competition and/or to buy our new product or service.

— The insights process.

— Let's explore a couple of these concepts briefly.

— Knowledge Management.

— The Voice of the Customer.

One of the ways the customer-centric organisation prevents any erosion of the customer-centric viewpoint is to structure its knowledge management around the voice of the customer. This is a simple concept: Any data that comes into the corporation from any field is further processed to represent knowledge of the customers their behaviour, attitudes, preferences, trends, and attributes. The emphasis here is that insights generation starts with customer data that is organised and accessible so that everyone in the organisation can locate, view, and cross-compare the latest data about customers, consumers, channels, and competitors.

Learning Plan

The second critical element of knowledge management for the insights generation process is the learning plan. Any data user can examine the voice-of-the-customer data and identify gaps in knowledge that the company doesn't have but needs. The user then submits a learning request. These learning requests are rolled up and prioritised. The prioritisation might be at the business unit level, the brand level, the country level, or the enterprise level, depending on the corporation's growth priorities. The corporation decides how much it wants to invest in learning this year, and the priority learning requests are fulfilled to the extent that the budget permits.

New learning is added to the voice of the customer and is circulated to subscribers so that they always have the most recent knowledge. As you will see in the steps of using value propositions and the corresponding financial pro forma, companies can make progress toward identifying a return on knowledge that will further refine their learning investment strategy.

Insights-Generation Tools

Insights don't come directly from data and analytics. They require what some technologists refer to dismissively as "wetware" human intervention. On the other hand, insights generation need not be feared as an inspirational "aha" moment that arrives only unpredictably via vintage-champagne-fueled musings of the super-creative guru. Wetware is not quite that wet. In fact, we have proven that insights generation can become a predictable, measurable, repeatable capability of the well-motivated and well-equipped team.

The insights workshop uses multiple principles of human dynamics. The first principle is that it's best to work via a cross-functional team representing multiple perspectives and expertise, using collaboration and accelerated interactive techniques to quickly generate, sort, and prioritise ideas. Another principle is that the best process involves small teams working together to generate ideas from one perspective. Then the teams come together in a large group to share those ideas and arrive at the next-generation synthesis. In turn, they go back to a small-team exercise, come back together in a large team to share and synthesise, and so on until one or two emerging "super solutions" are generated. Using this and other tools, our insights workshops have generated insights that consistently lead to profitable innovation.

The "six connects" tool is a good example of unleashing human creativity through technological enablement. This tool can easily be provided via an insights-generation software module and can be automated to some extent. The six connects are as follows:

— Connect behaviour to needs and emotions. *Examples*: Dove, iPod.

— Connect to consumer hopes and fears. *Examples*: Botox, Michelin.

— Connect heavy-usage data to emotional brand loyalty. *Example*: Gillette.

— Connect to insights used by others also targeting your consumer segment. *Example*: Coach benchmarking with spa marketers.

— Connect to experts. *Examples*: sociologists, anthropologists, psychologists, and market analysts.

— Connect to long-term trends. *Examples*: demographic changes, broad lifestyle changes, category trends, technology changes.

The "six connects" exercises start with the question "What behaviour (or non-behaviour) do I want to explain?" and conclude with an insights statement such as the following:

— The target group behaves in fashion X because of motivation Y. The opportunity to change/modify/enhance this behaviour is Z.

— An example is a target group of women who consider undergoing plastic surgery. Their motivation is that, as they get older, they believe that their attractiveness is impaired by the effects of aging. The consequence is that they feel a loss of self-esteem. To recover their attractiveness and self-esteem, they believe that an expert technological intervention is required. This opportunity is defined by the facts that this feeling is widely held and that the solution is limited by both its expense and risk. The delivery of a less-expensive but still-credible solution could create a new value stream among a much broader target group.

Value Proposition

Few value propositions are new. Most rebalance an existing value proposition and make it available to more users or enable more-frequent usage. The value proposition for plastic surgery comes from the same insight as the value proposition for Botox, but the Botox brand makes the solution more available to more women, who feel the same way as the surgery-users. When the perceived risk is lowered (both price and in-use risk), the same benefits become available to a broader audience.

Financial Pro Forma

From the value proposition, it's an easy step to the financial pro forma. How much revenue will this insight and its associated value proposition generate, and how much will it cost to commercialise? The downstream revenues can be estimated by identifying the number of users and the price per use. The calculation can be validated in various ways through modelling, surveys, research, and concept testing. How accurate are these estimates? At first, they will not be very accurate. But the act of making them can then generate a measurement tool, and the requisite skills and algorithms can be refined over time. You'll develop valuable intellectual property in the modelling and estimation of insights-based pro formas, which generates value in and of itself.

MARKETING CAPABILITY DEVELOPMENT

Training for marketers has come of age. No longer the preserve of studying for trade association exams or nodding off during lengthy PowerPoint presentations, a number of enlightened companies has realised that well-trained marketers can help boost the bottom line. A rigorous approach to improving the marketing effectiveness of a company by investment in building the capabilities of the whole marketing organisation is known as marketing capability development. Companies including Unilever, Hewlett Packard, Diageo, SABMiller, Tesco and BT are all investing to create a common marketing language, processes and tools and spreading examples of best practice across the organisation in order to drive growth with training being tied into addressing real business issues.

Crucially, marketing capability development goes well beyond conventional training, bringing tangible commercial benefits by teaching marketers to work more effectively. It is a strategic approach to people development that aims to build marketing excellence. Marketing capability development boosts the performance of a team or business as well as an individual, which means it is a potential driver for growth, rather than a cost.

3

DESIGNING OF EFFECTIVE MARKET PLAN

Many first-time business owners think that by simply placing an ad in a local newspaper or a commercial on a radio or a television channel, customers will automatically flock to purchase their product or service. This is true to a certain extent. Some people are likely to learn about your invention and try it, just out of curiosity. But hundreds, even thousands, of other potential customers may never learn of your business.

What you as a potential business owner must do is maintain a thorough understanding of your marketing programme, and use it to extract advantages from the market-place. Go over different strategies and techniques until you understand how to apply them to get the results you desire. Your aim is not only to attract and keep a steady group of loyal customers, but also to expand your customer base by identifying and attracting, new customers and to reduce risks by anticipating market shifts that can affect your bottom line.

To help you accomplish this aim, your marketing plan should include strategies typical of any marketing plan. The plan should especially include what marketers dub as the four P's of Marketing:

— Product
— Price
— Place
— Promotion

DESCRIBE YOUR PRODUCT

Try to describe the benefits of your products from your customer's perspective. Emphasise its special features—i.e., the selling points. Successful business owners know or at least have an idea of what their customers what or expect from them. This type of anticipation can be helpful in building customer satisfaction and loyalty.

DESCRIBE LOCATION (PLACE)

— description of the location
— advantages and disadvantages of location

Again, try to describe the location of your business from your customer's perspective. Describe its assets — i.e., the convenience, whether or not public transportation is accessible, the safety aspects—street lighting, well lit parking lot or facility, decor, etc. Your location should be built around your customers, it should be accessible and should provide a sense of security.

Develop Pricing Strategy

— pricing techniques and brief description of these techniques
— retail costing and pricing
— competitive position
— pricing below competition
— pricing above competition

— price lining
— multiple pricing
— material costs
— labour costs
— overhead costs

Although your pricing strategy may be based on the strategy devised by others, you should study this plan and the strategies used by competitors. That way you will acquire a thorough understanding of how to price your product, and you can determine if your prices are in line with competitors, if they are in line with industry averages and what adjustments you can make to bring them in line.

The key to success is to have an well-planned strategy, to establish your policies and to constantly monitor prices and operating costs to ensure profits. Keep abreast of changes in the market-place because these changes can affect your bottom line.

EFFECTIVE PROMOTIONAL STRATEGIES

— advertising media
— print media (newspaper, magazine, classified ads, Yellow Pages advertising, brochure)
— radio
— television
— networking
— business cards
— tee shirts, hats, buttons, pens

Develop a promotional strategy that uses various media for promoting your business. Monitor the different media identifying those that most effectively promote your business. Concentrate on developing material for these formats that clearly identifies your services, its location and price.

Since financial institutions weigh the soundness of your marketing plan when deciding whether your business is a good risk for their money, it is important that you prepare and present credible market data that shows there is a need in the community for your business and that demonstrates your ability to compete.

STRATEGIES OF MARKETING

Make certain it contains the strategies listed below and on the next page and then determine how these strategies will be applied by you.

Your target market:

— By age

— By sex

— By profession or career

— By income level

— By educational level

— By residence

Identify and describe your customers (target market) by their age, sex, income/educational levels, profession/career and residence. Know your customers better than you know anyone—their likes, dislikes, expectations. Since you will have limited resources target only those customers who are more likely to purchase your product. As your business grows and your customer base expands, then, you may need to consider modifying this section of the marketing plan to include other customers.

Identify Your Competition

— By market research data

— By demand for product
— By your nearest direct and indirect competitors
— By the strengths and weaknesses of competitors
— By an assessment of how competitors businesses are doing
— By a description of the unique features of your product
— By the similarities and dissimilarities between your product and competitor's
— By a pricing strategy for and comparison of yours and the competition's

Identify the five nearest direct competitors and the indirect competitors. Start a file on each identifying their weaknesses and strengths. Keep files on their advertising and promotional materials and their pricing strategies. Review these files periodically determining when and how often they advertise, sponsor promotions and offer sales.

Develop A Marketing Budget

— For your advertising and promotional plan
— For costs allocated for advertising and promotions
— For advertising and promotional materials
— For a list of advertising media to be used

Operating an effective marketing plan requires money, so you will have to allocate funds from your operating budget to cover advertising, promotional and all other costs associated with marketing. Develop a marketing budget based on the cost for the media you will use, and the cost for collecting research data and monitoring shifts in the market-place.

Advantages and Disadvantages of a Marketing Plan

A well-written, comprehensive marketing plan is the focal point of all business ventures because it describes how you plan to attract and retain customers, the most crucial aspect of a business. The marketing plan is essential to any successful business. It is the heart of the business, the basis from which all other operational and management plans are derived. Marketing offers you a wealth of information that if applied correctly virtually can ensure your success.

Therefore, it is important that you, as a first-time business owner, develop a comprehensive, effective marketing plan. An effective marketing plan will certainly boost your sales and increase your profit margins. You must be able to convince customers that you have the best product or service for them at the best possible price. If you cannot convince potential customers of this, then you are wasting your time and money. This is where the marketing plan comes into play, and this is why it is so important. There are numerous advantages you can extract from the market-place if you know how. And the marketing plan is an excellent tool for identifying and developing strategies for extracting these advantages.

Business advantages

- identifies needs and wants of consumers
- determines demand for product
- aids in design of products that fulfil consumers needs
- outlines measures for generating the cash for daily operation, to repay debts and to turn a profit
- identifies competitors and analyses your product's or firm's competitive advantage

— identifies new product areas
— identifies new and/or potential customers
— allows for test to see if strategies are giving the desired results

Business disadvantages

— identifies weaknesses in your business skills
— leads to faulty marketing decisions based on improperly analysed data
— creates unrealistic financial projections if information is interpreted incorrectly
— identifies weaknesses in your overall business plan

EFFECTIVE MARKETING PLAN

Now is good time to review what goes into a marketing plan. Write down what you can remember on a blank sheet and then compare it to this quick fact sheet. The marketing plan offers numerous advantages; however, as you can see, there can be drawbacks. Remember, however, the advantages outweigh the drawbacks, you can seek professional assistance when you are developing the marketing section of your business plan. It may be worth the investment.

How well your advertisements and promotions draw customers will ultimately determine how effective your marketing strategy is. It becomes your responsibility to cultivate your designated market, if you decide to market your invention yourself. One of the ways to do this is through advertising and promotions. Remember the aim of the advertising and promotional strategy is to create awareness of your product, to arouse customers' needs and expectations to the point of consumption and to create a loyal stream of satisfied customers who continue to patronise your business.

Effective Advertising and Promotional Strategy

Perhaps, the first step in developing an effective advertising and promotional strategy is to understand the difference between the two concepts. Most people think that advertising and promotions are one in the same; there is, however, a distinction between the two. While both advertising and promotions use the different media formats—print, radio, and television—as a way of conveying a message, promotion encompasses much more. It is the method of advertising and can entail community involvement.

For example, this could mean sponsoring a Youth Organisation, allowing non-profit organisations to use your facility, such as, letting the high school drama club use your parking lot for a car wash fund raiser, sending an underprivileged child to day camp or involvement in any type of positive community activity that will bring attention to your business. While advertising is a way of keeping your business is the public's eye, promotions are a way of signaling that you are concerned and committed to the welfare of the community and its residents. This commitment may be one of the most effective techniques for building customer loyalty. People tend to be more supportive of businesses and organisations that give something to the community rather than those that just take from the community, never giving anything in return.

Advertising plays an important role in successful business ventures. It entails identifying and selecting the media that provide the greatest amount of exposure for your business and developing effective, yet appropriate materials for each medium. It is more than running an ad in a local newspaper, on a radio or television channel or just simply hanging a sign outside your business and waiting for the customers to purchase your product. It requires that you know your product—that is, the selling points—and that you develop literature that can arouse the customers' consciousness levels to the point that they are curious enough to investigate it, and then raises their need or desire levels to the point that they are willing to purchase it.

Advertising keeps your product or service in the public's eye by creating a sense of awareness. Yet this awareness alone will not ensure the success of your business. Thus, advertising not only has to be effective, it also has to be a continuous process. It may be a good idea to mix the different media formats that you use. For example, design a brochure that describes your product, emphasising its selling points (special features). Place copies of the brochure in strategic locations of your business to use as customer handouts. Or, devise a customer survey.

The survey should focus on whether customers like the product, the quality of the product, ways to improve it, the quality of service provided by staff—their friendliness and courtesy. Place the survey with a self-addressed, stamped envelope near the check-out counter and ask customers to mail in or return the survey when they come back. Review their comments with staff and implement those suggestions that are practical, cost efficient and can improve the overall quality of service your business provides.

Media Formats

Newspaper, radio, or television ads (newspaper advertising is the least expensive and television advertising is the most expensive of these formats). You probably will need professional advice and assistance when developing ads for those media formats. The following media formats you probaly can do yourself:

— Business cards
— Classified ads in the local newspaper
— Direct marketing
— Telemarketing (this format can be expensive, also)
— Yellow Pages advertising
— Sampling—mailing or distributing free samples of your product to the public
— Advertising in community-based magazines or newspapers

Whatever media format you use, be willing to invest the money needed to develop an effective ad campaign.

Promotions

Promotion entails more than just selecting the media format to market your business. It can, and oftentimes does, encompass community involvement. This involvement can range from sponsoring a Boy or Girl Scout troop to hosting a charity ball for senior citizens or allowing non-profit organisations to use your facilities.

Your approach to promoting your business should encompass more than creating a sense of awareness about your business. It should include a commitment to community involvement—the desire to give something back to the community and its residents. An excellent way to foster this type of involvement is to meet with community leaders to find out how you can help, and what events are forthcoming that could or will require your assistance. Keep in mind that community leaders can be an excellent networking tool, especially if they feel your involvement is genuine.

MARKETING PLAN CAN DO

Even if you are not able to market your own invention,

writing a marketing plan will help you to sell or license your invention to manufacturers, retailers, and other interested parties. You will be able to intelligently discuss the market for your invention with potential buyers.

This tutorial on writing a marketing plan will provide you with the following marketing know-how:

— Understand the purpose of a marketing plan

- Identify strategies for conducting market research
- Identify advantages of market research
- Understand What The Marketing Plan Contains
- Target market
- Competition
- Product
- Marketing budget
- Location
- Pricing strategy
- Promotional strategy

— List

- Advantages of developing a marketing plan
- Disadvantages of developing a marketing plan

— Prepare A Marketing Plan Outline

— Develop An Effective Marketing Strategy

- Advertising strategy
- Promotional strategy

The key element of a successful marketing plan is to "know your customers", their likes, dislikes, and expectations.

You must also know your competition (or similar inventions) and their strengths and weaknesses. By identifying these factors, you can develop a marketing strategy that will allow you to arouse and fulfil customers needs, better understand competitors and identify changes in the marketplace.

The purpose of the marketing plan is to define your market, identify your customers and competitors, outline a strategy for attracting and keeping customers, and to identify and anticipate change. Again, even if you do not wish to market your own product having the above knowledge will impress both potential licensees and manufacturers.

Understanding the Marketplace

The first step in understanding the market is to study it through market research.

Through market research

— First write a description of your invention that a layperson would understand.

— When describing your product outline what you feel are its unique aspects, and explain how or why these aspects will appeal to customers.

— Emphasise the special features that you feel are its selling points.

— These features are what you will use to convince customers to purchase your product.

— Next go over sales projections, determining if there is a demand for the product or what the demand has been for similar products.

This practice will help you to better understand how the marketplace operates relative to your product, and it can help you develop the skills necessary to identify and anticipate changes in the market-place.

Marketplace trends

Start your own file on marketplace trends. Periodically review your data, looking for shifts in the market. If changes are occurring, you should modify your marketing plan to coincide with these changes.

A marketing plan should answer these questions

— Is this product in constant demand?

— How many competitors provide the same product?

— Can you create a demand for your product?

— Can you effectively complete in price, quality and delivery?

Review your marketing plan to ensure that it answers these questions. If your current marketing plan doesn't answer the questions, it will need to be modified. When you are satisfied that you understand how the marketplace operates relative to your invention. When you are satisfied that you understand how to identify market shifts and trends related to your inventions. You are ready to start writing the marketing plan section of your business plan.

Cultivating the marketplace

It is your responsibility to promote your invention by cultivating the marketplace, and by attracting and keeping customers. You can accomplish this aim by knowing your market, your customers, your competitors and your product. By gathering and analysing market research information, you will be better able to determine if your marketing plan is in line with your competitors, or if it is in line with industry averages and what adjustments you can make to improve your overall competitiveness.

STRATEGIES FOR RESEARCHING THE MARKET

Researching your market is perhaps your easiest way to conquer the market. Market research does not have to be costly, nor does it have to be a complex process. Market research can be as simple and as easy as surveying a cross-section of your consumers (focus group) to get their opinions about the invention that you will be offering, or conducting a telephone or mail survey. However, one disadvantage of using the telephone or mail survey method is that the individuals you contact may not be interested in responding to a survey.

Techniques for Market Research

Other market research techniques include:

— Analysing demographic data, such as population growth/decline rate; age range, sex, and income/ educational level.

— Brainstorming with family and friends

— Focus group interviews

Whatever method you use, your focus should be on gathering enough information to determine who your potential customers are, their needs, wants, and expectations; and if there is a demand for your product; who your competitors are and how well they are doing.

Market research should answer these Questions

— Who are your customers and potential customers?

— What kind of people are they?

— Where do they live?

— Can and will they buy the product you're offering?

— Are you offering the kinds of goods they want at the best place, the best time and best amounts?

— Are your prices consistent with what the buyers view as the products' values?

— Are you applying the promotional programmes in a way that will bring about success?

— Who are your competitors?

Advantages of Market Research

— Learning who your customers are and what they want.

— Learning how to reach your customer and how frequently you should try to communicate with them.

— Learning which appeals are most effective and which ones aren't.

— Learning the relative successes of different marketing strategies in relation to their return on investment.

While market research may appear to be a tedious, time-consuming process, it is often necessary if you want to be successful. Think of market research as simply a method of finding out what catches customers' attention by observing their actions and drawing conclusions from what you see or as an organised way of finding objective answers to questions every business owner and manager must answer in order to succeed.

Market research focuses and organises marketing information, ensuring that it is timely and that it provides what you need to:

— reduce business risks

— spot problems and potential problems in your current market

— identify and profit from sales opportunities

— and get basic facts about your markets to help you make better decisions and set up plans of action.

Market research is an invaluable tool that can save your time, effort, and money.

Disadvantages of Market Research

Market research is often a costly and time-consuming process. There may be biases that distort information, ignores answers or lets arrogance or hostility cut off communications at some point in the marketing process. The advantages, however, outweigh the disadvantages. Don't forego this process or stop halfway because you are not getting the desired results. This may be an indication that you are going with the wrong invention or that there isn't a market for your product. Don't be discouraged. You simply may need to modify your original marketing plan.

4

EFFECTIVE PRODUCT MARKETING

Once you see the presence of a problem that your product or service can solve, study that problem and reposition your marketing so that it is offering a benefit and a solution to that problem. You will notice that by doing this marketing and selling will become a lot easier.

Not sure if this works? Take a few moments and consider the products and services that are currently hot on the market. These products include products that help you quit smoking, lose weight, grow hair, and diminish wrinkles. Why are these products reaching a high level of success in sells? The answer is easy; they offer a benefit and a solution to a negative situation or problem.

Once you've identified the problem that your product or service solves, it's time to get to work by drafting your marketing material. When drafting your marketing plan be sure to mention the problem and the solution. This will assist your marketing efforts from going off in the wrong direction.

You will want to spend some time researching, problem-spotting, problem-discussing, and solution-positioning. The key to keeping your marketing efforts effective is to focus on selling the solution to the problem not selling the features or benefits.

YOUR CUSTOMER BEFORE MARKETING

Don't make the mistake of marketing your product or service before you've defined your customer or client. If you do, you're just throwing your marketing money away. Marketing isn't just a matter of placing ads. It's a method of attracting new business. Before you can hope to achieve this, you have to know exactly who you want to target with your marketing. You need to know your target market before you can reach them.

What's the point, for instance, in buying an advertising spot on TV if you're trying to sell whitewater rafting adventures? Are these sorts of people really going to be sitting in front of the tube? Define your customer by getting to know everything you possibly can about him or her. Think carefully about your product or service. Exactly who would want to purchase it? How old is this person? What is her marital status? Where does she live? How does she like to spend her spare time? What are her hobbies? What other products does she buy? Where does she go on vacation?

You need to develop your target market as specifically as possible if you're going to market your product or service effectively. So think of your "ideal" client or customer as a person. Visualise him or her in detail. "See" what he or she does, thinks, and wants.

If you can't visualise this person clearly and distinctly, then you need to research your potential customer or client until you can. Because until you can define your target market, you won't be able to make the decisions that need to be made about marketing, such as how, where, and when to advertise.

NEED MARKET RESEARCH

Anyone who's ever worked through a business plan

knows the answer to this one. Trying to start a small business without researching your potential market is as sensible as setting out for the North pole with a surfboard. But market research isn't just something you do when you're working on your business plan and then shelve. Market research needs to be an integral, ongoing part of your business' development.

It's crucial to analyse your market and target your clientele before you waste money on advertising that won't get you the results you want. Market research is also critical before you spend time and money developing a new product or service. Conducting market research essentially means gathering the information you need to make decisions about your business. Market research is the systematic gathering, recording, and analysing data relevant to selling the goods and/or services you produce.

There are a great many companies out there that will be glad to conduct paid market research for you. If, like many small business owners, hiring a company to do market research isn't in your budget, the rest of this article outlines how you can do your own market research, including tips for designing your own market research surveys and questionnaires. Continue on to the next page to learn about the basics of market research.

Doing your own market research isn't difficult, although it does tend to be time consuming. If you own a small business, you're probably researching your markets continually informally. Every time you talk to a customer about what he or she wants, or chat with a supplier or sales representatives, you're conducting market research.

But more formal market research is also necessary to keep your business vital and growing. There are so many companies in this field. The market research companies shows the two types of data sources and the three areas of research that are important to any business. You need to gather information from and about your customers to focus your marketing efforts, maintain and improve your customer service, and to guide your efforts in developing new products and/or services.

Looking at the market research companies, information gathered about the competition can help you determine what works and what hasn't worked, give you ideas for improving your products and/or services, and provide insight into how to increase or shift your share of the market.

The environment section of the market research companies refers to those economic, social, and political forces that shape business. Gathering information about the environment allows you to stay abreast of and respond to particular trends or events that impact your small business. Whether it's a predicted drop in interest rates, or the closure of a local mill, you need to be aware of it and judge the ripple effect on your business, for good or ill.

Think of secondary data sources as market research data that's already been collected by someone else. Telephone books, government publications, and sources such as, trade journals, and surveys conducted by other companies are all examples of information that's already been gathered that you can use to get a fix on what your customers want, what the competition has done, and what the environment is like.

Primary sources provide firsthand information. When you survey your customers or question the competition, you're gathering information directly from the source. While this kind of market research data can be the most costly and time-consuming to gather, it can also be the most valuable, because it's the most current and the most specific.

Tips for Doing Your Own Market Research

When you're doing your own market research, there are some things you should keep in mind.

1. *Your information will only be as good as your market research sample.* Be careful when selecting your market research sample group to question. To get useful market research data, your sample group needs to be relevant to and representative of your target population. That's because just asking people in the store isn't good enough. Some of them will say "Yes" just because they like me or don't want to offend me. Informal market research is always tainted to a degree by the relationships of the people involved.
2. *Design your survey or market research questionnaire carefully.* Make sure that it's focused specifically on the information you need to know, and that you haven't included any questions that may offend anyone. Many people are put off by questions that ask them how much money they earn, for instance. If you offend or confuse them, they won't bother to fill out your market research survey.
3. *Keep your survey or market research questionnaire fairly short.* If possible, your market research survey or questionnaire should all fit on one page. Some people are intimidated by long forms; others see multiple page forms as just too much of an imposition on their time.
4. *Always provide some opportunity for detailed answers.* Not everyone will take advantage of it, but some will, and sometimes these written-in comments are the most valuable of all.
5. *Work out your market research recording techniques first.* Telephone market research surveys are popular, but how are you going to record what the

respondents say? If you're orally interviewing someone, will you record them or take notes? The purpose of market research is to gather and analyse the data, so you've got to have a system of recording the data worked out in advance.

6. *Set the criteria for the information beforehand.* In other words, market research is a process, which may shut down or be redirected at any time.

Finding and Targeting Your Market

Finding target market

The most successful small businesses understand that only a limited number of people will buy their product or service. The task then becomes determining, as closely as possible, exactly who those people are, and 'targeting' the business's marketing efforts and dollars toward them. You, too, can build a better, stronger business, by identifying and serving a particular customer group – your target market.

One of the first things you need to do is to refine your product or service so that you are not trying to be 'all things to all people.' Next, you need to understand that people purchase products or services for three basic reasons:

— To satisfy basic needs.

— To solve problems.

— To make themselves feel good.

You'll need to determine which of those categories your product or service is the solution to, and be prepared to market it accordingly.

Your product or service may fit more than one category, too – our charter business primarily targets folks who just want to feel good – spending a day out on the water, relaxing and being waited on. But it also targets people who have visitors coming from out of town, or even overseas, because we represent a solution to the problem of "What will we do while our company is here? How can we entertain them, or show them our area?"

The next step in creating an effective marketing strategy is to zero in on your target market. Continue on to the next page to learn how to use market segmentation to define your target market.

Using market segmentation

Zero in on your target market by using Market Segmentation. First of all, is your product international or national in scope? Or is it more likely that you will sell it primarily in your own region or community? In the case of our charter business, our primary market is actually national or international – tourists who come to this area from all over the world. Our secondary market is local – people who have a special event to celebrate, a company meeting or retreat to plan, or company coming from out of town.

Let's say that your primary market is local or regional, and that you live in a community with a population of 25,000 people. The first thing you'll need to do is research the 'demographics' of your community, and divide it into market segments:

— *Age:* children, teens, young, middle, elderly

— *Gender:* male, female

— *Education:* high school, college, university

— *Income:* low, medium, high

— *Marital status:* single, married, divorced

— Ethnic and/or religious background

— *Family life cycle:* newly married, married for 10-20 years, with or without children.

This information should be available to you through your local town, hall, library, or Chamber of Commerce – and the more detail you can get, the better. Next, you need to segment the market as much as possible using 'psychographics' as your guide:

— *Lifestyle*: conservative, exciting, trendy, economical

— *Social class*: lower, middle, upper

— *Opinion*: easily led or opinionated

— *Activities and interests*: sports, physical fitness, shopping, books

— *Attitudes and beliefs*: environmentalist, security conscious.

In addition, you might want to find out how they purchase: seasonally, locally, only in volume, who makes the decisions? It is important to note that businesses, unlike individuals, buy products or services for three reasons only: to increase revenue, to maintain the status quo, or to decrease expenses. If you fill one or more of these corporate needs, you may have found a target market.

Lots of times prospective customers don't know about your company, or can't tell the difference between your company and others. It is your job, once you know who your best customers are, to 'target' the group that you've identified – even if you have competition.

5

BUSINESS ADVERTISING IDEAS

Advertising is the means of providing the most persuasive possible selling message to the right prospects at the lowest possible cost. In other words, having identified those customers whose needs and wants are best satisfied by your product or service, you evaluate the most costeffective method of communicating these benefits to them, thereby encouraging them to purchase from you.

At this stage, it is important to appreciate that advertising does not simply mean television, radio or newspapers. There is a wide range of techniques available, including:

— Advertising in directories

— Advertising in magazines

— Advertising in national newspapers (display or classified)

— Advertising in regional or local newspapers

— Advertising on television or in the cinema

— Advertising on commercial radio

— Poster advertising

— Direct mail

— Exhibitions
— Merchandising and point of sale
— Sales promotion
— Sponsorship
— Advertising through the Internet
— Mobile Communications

The most successful advertising is that which most effectively communicates with your customers. So, before beginning an advertising campaign, it is essential that you understand each of the above techniques in order that you can choose those most appropriate to your business needs. The basic discipline behind all sales, advertising or promotional activity is marketing.

SIGNIFICANCE OF QUALITY SERVICE

A popular extension to the 'Four Ps' is "Four Ps + One S". Here, the "S" stands for Service. The fate of any business often rests with its ability to provide quality service. Service begins before any sale is made, with good presentation, courtesy, efficiency and helpfulness. As customers yourselves, you know only too well how you take into account the treatment you receive before you buy. It is all about building up trust in your business and its products or services.

Everyone uses advertising, be it to look for a job, sell their house or find a car. We all also see hundreds of advertisements every day, so we are used to it being part of our lives. But how much do we remember? Ask someone to recall the ads they saw on television last night and they will struggle to remember more than a handful. Communication through advertising is by no means easy. However, because advertising is so familiar, people often think of themselves as experts.

The decision to advertise your products and services effectively is a very serious matter and requires careful planning and preparation. You must begin by asking yourself "what do I want my advertising to achieve?"

The first step is to analyse the benefits to your business that could be gained by advertising. Only when the objectives of the business are clear can the objectives of the advertising be established. For example, try to classify the goods or services you offer and set growth targets within each area over a fixed time period. Then categorise your audience within each of these areas into existing customers and potential new customers. By completing even this simple exercise, you will be in a better position to begin compiling a marketing and advertising plan.

By way of illustration, we suggest you try the simple exercise shown below. Simply tick those statements which best apply to your business today:

1. People who always buy from a competitor and don't know us.
2. People who buy from a competitor, know us but have never bought from us.
3. People who mainly buy from a competitor, but know us and buy from us occasionally.
4. People who mainly buy from us, but occasionally from our competitors.
5. People who buy from us and never from our competitors.

The conclusion that can be drawn from the above exercise is that different types of advertising may be required. Advertising needs to be tailored to its precise audience because it is wasteful to try to communicate to all audiences with equal effort. No single advertising message will appeal to all targets, so hard decisions have to be taken as to which target offers most potential.

Examples of Advertising Messages

1. An advertisement designed for nonusers who don't know you or your products, stimulating an initial interest.
2. An advertisement designed to make existing customers buy more often from you and less from a competitor, in other words developing loyalty.
3. An advertisement designed to offer customers something better than your competitors can, encouraging change.
4. An advertisement designed to reassure existing loyal customers that they are making the right choice buying from you, encouraging them to remain loyal.

It is important to understand that even with careful analysis, advertising remains a matter of judgement rather than science. However, you can improve your judgement by increasing your knowledge of your industry, your business and, most importantly, your customers.

Knowing your Customer

At the heart of many business decisions is the need to know your customer. However good your product or service, it will ultimately fail unless it is what your customer wants or needs. Thousands of new products from large companies are launched every single year. Many of them have advertising budgets running into millions of pounds. Significantly, a number of these products fail because nobody wanted them or was persuaded to try them. The huge sums spent on their development, manufacture, distribution and, ultimately, advertising could have been saved if only the initial idea had been tested using careful market research.

BENEFITS OF MARKET RESEARCH

Careful and accurate market research is essential to any business. It can provide vital information, all of which will help you:

- — Identify customers
- — Increase sales
- — Improve products and services in line with customer requirements

Desk Research

Desk research is the study of existing information. There is a wealth of literature available, from a range of sources, much of which is either inexpensive or available free. Here are a few examples:

- — *Trade and professional magazines:* These frequently publish surveys and reports on the market or the consumer.
- — *Media owners:* Newspaper and magazine publishers produce data on their readers, circulations and advertising rates. This is available free of charge. Don't forget, their ultimate aim is to sell you advertising space.
- — *Specialist organisations:* There ae so many organisations—Trade associations, the Advertising Association. Tata Yellow pages publish useful information. Trade directories are often available for study in your local Business or Reference Library.
- — *Government:* Statistics detailing the economic environment, e.g. regional employment levels and income trends, are normally available at business and reference libraries.

Field Research

Field research involves obtaining your own information, through direct contact with your chosen audience. This service is most effectively carried out by a market research consultancy for which fees would be charged. However, there is no substitute for high quality information. The advantage of employing an external researcher is their independence. Your customers are more likely to be honest with a third party. They may not be comfortable criticising you to your face, in which case their contribution would be inaccurate and, therefore, misleading.

However, if you cannot afford specialists, you can easily carry out valuable field research yourself. For example:

— Why do existing or new customers choose to buy from you?

Ask telephone enquirers how they heard of your business.

or Telephone your customers and ask them for their opinions.

or Enclose a simple questionnaire and an s.a.e. with their bill.

or arrange a customer 'open evening' and use it to gather information.

— Always ask direct questions

People do not respond effectively to openended questions like do you have any comments? Think of exactly what you want to know and ask it outright.

— Consider offering incentives

You want as many people to respond as possible, because the more information you have, the more accurate your conclusions will be. Consider prize draw entries or modest discounts for customers who return the information you request,

— Involve your team

Encourage your staff to let you know what customers say to them, good or bad. Arrange a regular meeting to do this or provide them with a book to log customer comments.

How Advertising Works

We all take in huge amounts of information every day. Before we leave home, we may talk with our families, receive mail, read a newspaper, watch television or listen to the radio. Advertising is just one element of this mass of information, so it has to work very hard to compete for our attention. It is easy to overestimate the power of your advertisement and expect too much. Whilst there is no doubt that good and appropriate advertising does work, there are numerous factors to consider when investing in advertising:

— Advertising is persuasive not coercive: it cannot make people do what they do not want to do.

— Advertising has to be seen by its intended audience: so using the appropriate medium is essential.

— The audience has to be receptive: they must have an interest in your message.

— The message has to be driven home: a single advertisement may be missed or forgotten.

— Competitors advertise too: your offer must be better or different, otherwise why choose you?

The hardest fact to accept is that most people ignore most advertising. The key is to ensure that they take notice of yours. There are a number of reasons why people find certain advertising memorable, for example:

— *They recognise your company or its products/services:* People like what they know. Regular advertising builds awareness.

— *They have company or product loyalty:* Existing customers have a relationship and take notice of what you do.

— *They are actively seeking to purchase:* Your product or service is something they have already decided they need.

— *They are "in the market":* Your product or service is something they are considering purchasing.

— *The "offer" is attractive:* Your advertising contains a positive incentive to purchase (e.g. a free gift with the purchase or a price reduction).

Good advertising works because it puts the company, its products and its messages at the forefront of people's minds. It either stimulates an early purchase, or helps to ensure that people know where to go when they do decide to purchase. The final point to consider is tell people what to do next.

Where to Advertise

Once you have identified your target audiences, you need to communicate with them either directly (verbally or in writing) or indirectly through an advertising medium. When choosing where to advertise, you must identify those publications, broadcast media or other methods which offer the best 'fit' with your target audiences. It may be appropriate to use different media and different messages. However, before you decide, you must understand what is available.

Direct Marketing

Direct marketing is one of the most accountable forms of advertising media, since both costs and results can be measured precisely. It also assists with customer relations by building a twoway dialogue, thereby helping you to understand customer needs and expectations.

Direct marketing includes such disciplines as direct mail, mail order, direct response advertising i.e. television, radio and press advertising which invites an immediate telephone or written response and telemarketing, where existing or potential customers are contacted by telephone. Of these, currently the most widespread is direct mail.

Research with statistics show that direct mail is both appreciated and effective:

— The average householder responds to direct mail three to four times every year.

— 43% of business people consider the direct mail they receive to be 'very useful' or 'quite useful'.

— 58% expect companies who trade with them to mail them when they have a special offer available.

— 50% would like to be mailed whenever a company they already do business with has a new product or service available.

— 55% would like to be mailed whenever a company they already do business with has new literature available.

Ingredients for Success

There are three main aspects to a direct mail campaign that will affect its success.

1. *The mailing list:* The best mailing list is the one that contains the most potential purchasers. This would

normally include existing or previous customers. The difficult part is including potential new customers. If you know what you want, you can also choose to go to a list owner or have your own unique list compiled by a list builder.

2. *The proposition:* The proposition is the offer that you can make that will encourage recipients to respond. It must answer the question 'what's in it for me?'

   Accuracy of your information will influence how people react. Make sure all names and facts are correct. Information about your company, its products and its reputation will build confidence. Simplify the response mechanism, ideally by enclosing a post-paid, self-addressed envelope. Make them an offer, it is important you make clear the real reason why you are writing.

3. *Creativity of the mailing:* Creativity in direct mail is a means to an end. The use of stylish graphics, professional copywriting or photography should be used to achieve that predetermined objective. Just as job candidates are expected to be well presented, so a "welldressed" mailing is more likely to be read and appreciated than one that looks 'cobbled together'.

   Stylish, relevant design grabs and holds the attention. Literate, well structured copy increases readership and response. Finally, direct mail does not end when you receive a response. Monitor all replies, fulfil orders promptly, update your database for reuse, notify suppliers and staff of any action required from them, spot check respondents to make sure they are satisfied with the followup service and finally and most importantly, maintain contact in the future.

THE PRESS

In India, the press, by which we mean newspapers, magazines and periodicals, is the most widely used advertising medium, accounting for around 50% of all advertising expenditure. One of the reasons for this volume is that the press is so diverse, including all the following and more:

- — National daily newspapers
- — National Sunday newspapers
- — Regional daily newspapers
- — Regional weekly newspapers
- — Local free distribution newspapers
- — General interest magazines
- — Special interest magazines
- — Trade, technical and professional magazines
- — House magazines
- — Yearbooks and reference journals

In total there are thousands of publications. The great advantage of such a selection is that it is possible to target specific audiences with particular interest in your business. In simple terms, national newspapers offer extremely high circulation, wide coverage and the ability to target demographically and by region. They are ideal for advertising general consumer goods.

Press Advertising

1. Flexibility

The press offers such variety and scope that it is possible to target specific groups of readers on a national, local or special interest basis. You can segment your audience by sex, age, income group, business or hobby.

Advertisements can be purchased and designed at very short notice. It is possible to use colour, illustrations or photographs to enhance your message and reply coupons can usually be incorporated within the design. In the daily press you can even relate an advertisement to a current news story.

Also advertisements can be booked to appear in a given issue, in a given place within the title, such as opposite the television page or within the new products section.

These options naturally all have different prices. Special positions and full colour or spot colour insertions all carry premium charges.

If you don't mind where your advertisement appears, it will be placed run of paper, which means anywhere available. This costs less but you have no control over where it appears.

2. The power of the written word

A press advertisement can be used to convey a broad message or to contain very precise and detailed information. The space is available to tell a story, build up an image and present your case to your customer. Once you have booked your space, you have complete control over what is said, how it is said and, if you choose a special position, where it is said.

3. Cost-effectiveness

If you identify the right titles for your business, with the lowest levels of 'wastage' in the readership (readers who would not be interested in your product/service), press advertising will prove to be a highly efficient method of reaching your audience at what is a comparatively low cost per prospect.

One key consideration when using press, which may influence your advertising decisions, is the measurement of readership, as well as circulation. Readership figures are higher than circulation figures, as they relate to the number of people who see the publication, rather than the number of copies bought (circulation). These figures need to be identified when possible. The National Readership Survey can help.

4. Measurable Response

Because, as mentioned earlier, you can include response coupons and/or telephone hotlines within your advertisement designs, it is possible to judge accurately the success of each publication. This not only helps you process today's responses, it also enables you to plan your future advertising based upon proven performance data.

RADIO

Commercial radio is available to advertisers on a local and national basis either through the national sales houses or your local station. It is a source of information, entertainment and companionship to millions of people and typically provides a backdrop to other activities for lengthy periods, e.g. driving or domestic tasks.

In any fourweek period, over 80% of 15 to 50 year olds listen to Commercial Radio. The majority of these listeners have their radio permanently tuned into their favourite station, which they listen to at the same times each day.

Radio listeners are loyal and people relate to their favourite programmes and presenters. Radio is most popular outside peak television viewing hours, with breakfast time (6 am to 9 am) and evening drive time (5 pm to 6 pm) being the periods of heaviest listening.

The use of Radio depends very much upon the overall objectives of the advertising campaign. Radio is an excellent medium for those wishing to build familiarity, accessibility and involvement with the product or service. The loyalty with the medium is subconsciously transferred to the advertiser. There is also the option of sponsorship of programmes.

Use of Radio Advertising

1. *The Impact of sound:* The human voice is a powerful selling aid. It can convey emotion and authority and, when backed by music, can attract attention or create atmosphere. The onetoone nature of the medium, reinforced by its local content, makes it intensely personal for the listener. A good radio station mirrors its audience and the moods conveyed by sound can prove very memorable.

   Local radio stations are part of the community and, as such, benefit from being extremely close to their listeners

2. *Flexibility:* A radio is portable and can be listened to anywhere and whilst doing other things. Programming is designed to target distinct audiences. Pop music shows appeal to a high proportion of younger people, whilst chat shows may reach a slightly older, more predominantly female audience and sports coverage tends to increase the male listening figures. Your advertising can be broadcast to coincide with, and capitalise upon, these variations.

   Radio advertising is usually quick and easy to produce. This, coupled with the fact that radio is live, immediate and topical, allows you to add urgency and importance to your message.

3. *Low cost:* Radio advertising space, known in the business as air time, can be purchased in packages which offer a relatively inexpensive option. The cost of writing and recording of advertisements can also be attractive and stations will often incorporate this within their package deals.

   Commercial messages can benefit from this intimacy and trust. However, creativity is essential. Radio advertisements are short and the listener's attention is immediately drawn to the next item. Likewise, there is no visual support for your message. The script must therefore be catchy, strong and, above all, memorable. If all these factors are addressed, the radio can be a highly successful advertising medium.

TELEVISION

Television is regarded by many as the single most powerful advertising medium available. This is partly because, over 70% of the population watch television every day. According to a survey commercial television viewing accounts for over 50% of this total. It now includes cable and satellite options.

Use of Television Advertising

The benefits of television advertising are clear from these figures. The audience is massive and captive. By repeating advertisements many times, known in the business as frequency, it is possible further to increase this audience and secure more effective total coverage.

Television can be used tactically, e.g. locally, regionally or nationally, and effectively targeted. Sophisticated data on the habits of viewers is available, enabling the advertiser to identify the particular audience profile. In production terms, the medium offers moving pictures and high quality sound, enabling exceptional creativity to be brought into play by advertisers. Messages can be presented extremely powerfully.

Television advertising is extremely costeffective for the right type of advertisers, but this does not mean it is inexpensive. Thirty seconds of prime time, costs many lacks of rupees. However, given the millions of people watching, the relative cost of reaching each one of them is low. In addition, production costs can be substantial. The most effective method of securing value for money is to produce an advertisement of such quality and longevity that it is used many times over many months or years.

CINEMA

There are thousands of cinema screens in India. Maximum people visit the cinema at least twice a month or at least once every two to three months.

Use of Cinema Advertising

Cinema audiences are captive, attentive and usually appreciative. The cinema is an experience, consisting of many elements from 'previews to popcorn' and the advertising is very much part of this total entertainment package. Cinemas do not offer distractions. The auditoriums are dark and the audience is largely silent. Attention levels are unrivalled and advertising messages are usually watched, listened to and absorbed within the cinema environment.

Advertising that uses sound and vision is displayed to its best possible effect through the use of the big screen and sophisticated sound technology.

Cinema advertising time can be purchased locally, regionally or nationally. It may also be linked to certain categories of film, e.g. 18 certificate or children's, or even to specific film titles. All this allows the smaller, local advertisers to appear on the big screen at very affordable rates.

Production costs, using the facilities offered by the major cinema advertising contractors, are surprisingly low.

Again, this opens the door on cinema to the smaller advertiser.

When considering cinema advertising, it is important to obtain as much audience data as possible, in order to ensure that your products/services and messages are consistent with the particular sector of the cinemagoing public you will reach when you purchase advertising.

Directories

Directories are a useful advertising medium because they are so highly focused. There are so many directories in India, approximately 50% of which are industrial and commercial titles, aimed at specific sectors and well used by them.

Industrial and commercial directories such as Yellow Pages are almost totally used by those who are predisposed to purchase.

They invariably have a long shelflife, typically a full year and are almost always seen by potential buyers only when they are ready to buy. Directories are specific reference publications and not reading matter for the casual browser Directory advertising is not seen as an overt sales pitch. The publication provides information, not promotion, and is vital to the customer who is actively seeking the advertiser. For this reason, they are an ideal support medium, providing relevant details to an already captive audience.

OUTDOOR ADVERTISING

Outdoor advertising is a diverse medium, appearing in many shapes and sizes. Some of the more popular forms are listed below:

— *Poster advertising:* Such as the massive sites on roadsides, to small, wallmounted sites and the ends of bus shelters.

— *Station advertising:* Posters appearing in airports, train stations and bus terminals.

— *Onboard advertising:* Smaller posters appearing on trains, underground trains, buses and in taxis.

— *Sides and supersides:* Posters and even individual paintwork appearing on buses and taxis.

— *Mobile advertising:* Lorries and trucks which are specifically built to carry mobile poster sites.

Use Outdoor Advertising

Posters (are normally sited in high traffic areas, which can be mobile or pedestrian. Therefore, each individual poster has a high opportunity to see rating.

Poster sites can be cost effectively purchased locally, regionally or nationally.

Poster advertising provides an excellent trigger at or near the point of purchase, e.g. in a busy shopping centre or high street. It can therefore be used to make very specific announcements, such as opening soon on this site.

By its nature, Poster advertising cannot be acted upon immediately. People see posters as they pass by. This means the messages have to be very short and easy to digest. Their most effective use is therefore as a reminder, keeping a product or service in the mind. For this reason, Poster advertising is universally accepted as being a highly effective support medium, reminding the audience of other forms of advertising for the same product/ service, e.g. press or television campaigns.

CREATIVE ADVERTISING

The quality of each advertising message obviously plays a key role in its success. Creative advertising offers many benefits and helps you to meet your overall objectives, by:

— Gaining the attention of the audience

— Capturing their imagination

— Opening their minds to your sales messages

— Differentiating your products and services from all others

— Giving them a reason to choose you

— Adding value to your products and services

— Helping the audience to remember

Being creative is one of the most difficult areas of advertising. You must accept that one man's meat is another man's poison, which brings us back to knowing your customers. Fortunately, the preparation of creative and effective advertising is an area where you can get lots of help. These experts have developed some tips which you can use when compiling your own ads:

1. *Match your medium to your audience:* People who see your advertising must be interested in what you have to sell.
2. *Play for position:* When advertising in the press, convention has it that early pages are best (with the exception of outside covers and specific special positions). It is also believed that right hand pages receive more attention. The point is, think about where you want to be and make sure you're there.
3. *Size does matter:* People are more likely to see your advertisements if they are large.

4. *All things bright and beautiful:* Research shows that people not only notice colour advertising, they are also more likely to read something that is bright and eyecatching.
5. *Every picture tells a story:* Psychologists have proved that people have an almost unlimited capacity for remembering visual images. Pictures show things as they truly are.
6. *Hit the headlines:* Take your key statement and turn it into a concise headline. It doesn't have to be witty, but it must never be clumsy or unclear.
7. *Watch your words:* Make one or two strong claims and support them with evidence. Give your audience a reason to buy, visit, call or try.
8. *Sign off with style:* Summarise your philosophy and your offer in one, concise line. 'We care because you do' says it all for Boots.
9. *Make yourself easy to choose:* Always include your name, address, telephone number, email, web site and, if appropriate, brief directions and hours of business.

Above all, make sure your advertising stands out from the crowd!

TESTING YOUR ADVERTISING

It is always desirable to test the effectiveness of your advertising. In order to develop ideas or campaigns that work for you, you need to evaluate the reactions of your audience and, possibly, alter your advertising accordingly.

Testing Methods and Ideas

Ideally, several different approaches should be tried to measure relative success. Advertisements should be placed in different areas of your chosen medium, in order that the most effective timings, editions or positions can be established. Coupons and telephone hotlines will enable you accurately to monitor response. If you advertise widely, give each individual advertisement a code number relating to the date and place it appears. You can also run different advertisements to test cost effectiveness.

Key elements in testing

1. *Time:* Give each test long enough to produce worthwhile results.
2. *Organisation:* Plan your testing schedules and methods and stick to them.
3. *Investment:* Some advertising techniques will prove unsuccessful. Don't give up: an effective advertising campaign is worth every penny.
4. *Thought:* Know your customers. When, where and why do they want your products or services. If you're not sure, keep testing.

ADVERTISING AGENCY

Advertising agencies specialise in the planning, design, production and media buying of campaigns on behalf of client companies who advertise. They provide indepth knowledge of the disciplines involved in marketing and advertising, together with the creative inspiration required to develop effective ideas.

As with all business services, such as legal advice or accountancy, their expertise costs money. Fees vary depending upon type and volume of work and the calibre of personnel involved. However, if they achieve measurable results, their fees will be outweighed by the additional income they generate.

There are so many agencies in through-out India. You may contact them and ask them to send you details of how they work and some examples of their current work. They will do this freely and without obligation.

Selecting an Advertising Agency

As in most areas of business, initial meetings are free. Agencies will gladly provide a credentials' presentation, during which they will guide you through work carried out for existing clients. At this stage, you should ask about costs and whether the agency works on a fixed fee, an ad hoc fee, or a commission basis. Having met them, how impressed you are with what you see and hear will help you decide how impressed your audience might be with the work they do for you.

If you cannot decide on this basis, you should invite a selection of agencies (usually no more than three) to compete for your business. This is known as a pitch. You must prepare and issue a brief, specifying what you wish to achieve and inviting them to present a strategy and creative ideas for your business. Remember to insist that each agency outlines how they plan to monitor advertising effectiveness. Once appointed, they have to be prepared to be judged on the basis of results. Finally, you should specify a budget, as this has a major impact upon the approaches recommended.

Some agencies will not present ideas without receiving a pitching fee. You should not discriminate against them because of this basis, as it means they are unwilling to increase their overheads to existing clients by seeking new work for themselves. If you become their client, you will appreciate this loyal approach. When the agencies present their proposals, you will then be in a position to choose your agency based upon work they have prepared for you.

6

HOW TO DEVELOP YOUR BRAND

A brand is a "name, term, sign, symbol or design, or a combination of them intended to identify the goods and services of one seller or group of sellers and to differentiate them from those of other sellers. Therefore it makes sense to understand that branding is not about getting your target market to choose you over the competition, but it is about getting your prospects to see you as the only one that provides a solution to their problem.

The objectives that a good brand will achieve include:

— Delivers the message clearly

— Confirms your credibility

— Connects your target prospects emotionally

— Motivates the buyer

— Concretes User Loyalty

To succeed in branding you must understand the needs and wants of your customers and prospects. You do this by integrating your brand strategies through your company at every point of public contact.

Your brand resides within the hearts and minds of customers, clients, and prospects. It is the sum total of their experiences and perceptions, some of which you can influence, and some that you cannot.

A strong brand is invaluable as the battle for customers intensifies day by day. It's important to spend time investing in researching, defining, and building your brand. After all your brand is the source of a promise to your consumer. It's a foundational piece in your marketing communication and one you do not want to be without.

OBJECTIVES OF YOUR BRAND

Critical to effective brand management is the clear definition of the brand's audience and the objectives that the brand needs to achieve. What are the objectives that you hope to achieve with your brand?

Your brand should be comprised of the company personality, image, core competencies and characteristics. The impressions that you make as well as the words people will use to describe your company to others, are the basic framework of your brand.

With a strong brand you build credibility, have more influence on your market, and motivate customers and clients to purchase from you.If done correctly your company will be looked at as a leader not a follower.

To determine your brand objectives ask yourself the following questions:

— What is it that you want your brand to do for your company?

— What do you want others to know and say about your products or services?

Sample objectives may include:

— Being recognised by receiving a specific award

— Picking up a certain number of choice projects

— Gaining a specific number of new clients in the next year
— Positioning your company as an industry leader in the next five months

You will find that by defining your objectives with specifictimelinesit is easier to develop a plan of action to achieve those objectives.

By defining your objectives you are able to map out a plan on how to achieve those objectives. Say for example your objective is to position your company as an industry leader. How can you go about doing this? You could:

— Have members of your team speak at Trade Shows
— Schedule lectures at professional group gatherings within your industry
— Write and publish articles in newspapers, magazines, or online media.

Once you've determined your objectives the next step is to build and develop your brand strategy by listing out how, when, and what you are going to do to accomplish and meet your those brand objectives. Use the questions above to determine your brand objectives. List each objective and map out how you plan to accomplish and succeed in meeting those objectives.

YOUR TARGET AUDIENCE

Your value proposition must be relevant to your target market. This means your target market must be clearly defined. It's not uncommon for a business to have to refocus and revisit their targeting, especially if it was not clearly identified in the beginning stages of business. It is necessary to find the right balance when defining your target market in a way that causes your audience to recognise that you are talking specifically to them. This often requires companies to narrow down their target market.

It does not matter what your Brand mission is identifying and gaining the devotion of your target audience is the necessary means to reaching those objectives. To achieve your brand marketing goals it is important that you know your target market inside and out.

This requires conducting a market analysis. This market analysis must be as in-depth as possible providing you will all the data you need to reach your target effectively. By knowing your target audience you will be more confident in the steps to take to connect with that audience.

The power of your brand relies on the ability to focus. That is why defining your target market will help to strengthen your brand's effectiveness.

There are two steps in developing your brand's strategy. The first is to conduct and informal market analysis of your target market and the second is to write a target audience definition for your company. The instructions below will walk you through the process of completing both of these steps.

Your Informal Market Analysis

The following questions will help you assess your market analysis. Make your study as complete as possible. Use the Internet to conduct research. You can also read news stories that are related to your target market. This will help you to narrow down your target by interest, demographic, and common trends.

— Who is your target audience?

— Where is your target audience located?

— What do they think about your current brand?
— What would you like them to think about your brand?
— How will you attract them to your products or services?
— Who else is competing for their loyalty and devotion?
— Are you targeting business or consumer sectors?

Write Your Target Market Description

When creating your brand strategy for a product or service it is important to perform a careful analysis to determine principal barriers that you may come in contact with. These barriers are also known as market conditions that can keep your product or service from achieving success.

For example they could include the following:

— Competition
— Timing
— Financing
— Location
— Lack of Demand

In order to be prepared to face these obstacles or barriers it is important to spend time doing a careful analysis of your product or service. This analysis will assist you not only in the development of your brand, but also in the positioning of your product or service.

A careful and thorough analysis will assist you in answering the following questions:

— Do you have a niche market? What problem does your product or service solve or need?

— How should you determine the price of your product or service?

— Who are your potential customers and where can you find them?

— Who are your biggest competitors? What can you do better than them?

— How should you advertise? Where will you find your target market? Will you use new media or traditional media?

Now that you have your questions where do you start your market analysis research? Starting your research is actually easier than you think, but it will take time.

You will need to dedicate hours to this research in order for it to be useful and effective.

Keep informed on current market conditions and trends in your vertical market by subscribing to trade publications, news alerts, and electronic newsletters.

BRAND PACKAGING

Branding is your identity in the marketplace, is yours saying what it should? Your company image is all about the appearance of your packaging. What is your company image saying to the marketplace?

It's important to realise that packaging always either has a negative or positive influence on the purchaser. A negative impression can detour a potential customer, just as a positive reaction can influence a customer to buy. A time to pay special attention to your packaging is when you are in the launch of a "new" brand. If you've already built a strong brand that others recognise often people may not pay as close attention to the packaging.

How can you package your brand so that it is an integral part of your business and represents a strong identity? Packaging can be judged and represented by the following common business tools:

— business cards and stationery

— web site

— answering system

— email address

What image are you putting across with these business tools that you use everyday? What are they saying about your company? Take a few moments and lets look at each one of these. What are your business cards and stationery saying? Are they saying we are strong, we are confident, and we can succeed in helping you? Or does it reflect an image that says we are flimsy, our dynamics are minimal, and we will try but we cannot guarantee continuity?

What does your web site say about your company? Does it reflect professionalism, clarity, and show them that you respect and care about them? Or does your web site confuse viewers, project an untrustworthy image of your company and ultimately drive potential customers away?

What does your answering system and call return policy say about your company? Does it say we are here to help, eager for you business and will do what it takes? Or is it putting across the message that you are too busy to cater to new clientele, don't care about their needs, and wish they would just quit calling?

What does your email address say about your company? Does it suggest your role in the company, is it easy to remember, and does it something about you and your business? As you can see all these things speak volumes about your image and they either strengthen or weaken your brand. Your image is all in the packaging. Would potential clients take a second look or is your message getting lost? If you thought these things were not worth the investment or didn't matter, you were wrong. Clients and customers will make assessments of your company based on these things and while not always conscious, that customer appraisal says much about your business, your attitude and your priorities.

Creating Logo and Tag Line

Have you ever asked yourself why a competitor's business gets more attention than yours? The answer just may have to do with the elements that go into how memorable the business is. And that has to do with branding.

But exactly what is branding, anyway? Think of branding as predefining what a company is all about in the minds of its clients. Good branding differentiates your products and services in a positive way that really sticks in the minds of potential customers.

Let's say you are getting ready to run errands on a busy Saturday morning, thinking about the groceries that need to be bought, the dry cleaning that needs to be picked up, and the packages that must get to the post office before noon. The trip to the post office reminds you that your favourite aunt's birthday is next Wednesday.

You need to add buying and mailing a birthday card to your list of things to do. Without a moment's hesitation, you know exactly where you will buy the card: the local Archives gallery. Why did you think Archives?

The answer to that question has everything to do with Archive's branding and two key elements of that branding are:

— a logo design that's attractive, easy to read and memorable;

— a great tag line.

Assuming your own product is fabulous, it all comes down to image. Graphic design can play a huge part in that image. But what are some key things to consider?

Create a Great Logo

You have given a great deal of attention to your company name and believe it speaks to who you are and what you do. Great! Now you need to wrap a graphic image around that name to carve out a prime piece of real estate in your target customer's mind. That is exactly what a great logo design can do.

Tips to Logo Design

Keep in mind that a powerful logo design:

— has a strong, balanced image with no little extras that clutter its look;

— is distinctive and bold in design, making it easy to see at a glance;

— has graphic imagery that looks appropriate for your business;

— works well with your company name;

— is done in an easy to read font;

— communicates your business clearly; and

— looks good in black and white, as well as in colour.

Archive's memorable crown logo is one of the reasons that Archvies comes to mind so quickly when you need to buy a greeting card. It is simple, bold, looks good in either colour or black and white, and bespeaks the quality required for something to be stamped with a Archives, so it works well with the company name. While the image might not have communicated the nature of the business when it was first created, it certainly does now!

Create a Distinctive Tag Line

A tag line is a three to seven word phrase that accompanies your logo. It expresses your company's most important benefits and/or what you want your customers to remember about working with you. Think of it as the words you want to linger in your target customer's mind about you and what you have to offer.

Great tag lines appear to be effortlessly created because they just seem to flow. In fact, creating and refining one takes time, just like designing a great logo. The benefits of taking the time to craft a great tag line lie with the tag line's stickiness. Great tag lines stick in your memory.

The Hallmark company was founded by J. C. Hall, so the name Hallmark was a natural. It was also brilliant from a marketing standpoint. Archives cards have been used for decades as a stamp to denote quality, purity, and genuineness. Could there be a better way to attach the image of quality to a product? The tag line capitalises on that image well with words that stick in the mind and exemplify good taste.

Creating a great logo and distinctive tag line are critical in creating a brand that provides the perfect image for your company and great ones just might be memorable enough to give your company the beach front property in the minds of your customers that leaves them thinking only of you.

STEPS TO BRAND BUILDING

Touchpoints

Customers experience your brand in numerous ways: products, packaging, price, marketing, sales personnel, etc. Each of these contacts or touchpoints molds the customer's impression of the brand. Some of these touchpoints are obvious, like product performance, and one-on-one customer interactions. Other touchpoints, such as the product manual, monthly statements or post-sales support, may be subtler in their brand effects.

Your brand image creates expectations. It defines who you are, how you operate, and how you're different from your competitors. In essence, your brand image is a promise—a promise that must be kept.

If the brand is a promise you make, then the customer experience is the fulfilment of that promise. The customer experience can't be left to chance. It should be actively designed and controlled in a manner that enhances your brand image. It must consistently reinforce the brand promise across every customer touchpoint or the value of the brand itself is at risk.

Here are five easy steps to building a strong brand and an optimised customer experience:

1. Identify your reasons-to-believe

Your brand promise is irrelevant if your customers do not believe it. Therefore, your promise must be supported by reasons-to-believe. This will automatically add substance to the promise and define specific expectations for the customer.

For example, an automobile manufacturer promises potential customers that Car XYZ is an "intelligent choice for serious drivers." What makes it an intelligent choice? Why should the customer believe this promise? To address this question effectively, the manufacturer could frame its promise with two reasons-to-believe... sporty performance and safety. These two reasons in essence define "intelligent choice" and clearly set customer expectations. They also give the company specific direction for designing the customer experience through tangible customer touchpoints like vehicle design features, advertising campaigns, dealer sales approaches, and customer service activities.

2. Identify customer touchpoints

Each individual step in your business process contains a number of touchpoints when the customer comes in contact with your brand. Your ultimate goal is to have each touchpoint reinforce and fulfil your marketplace promise.

Walk through your commercial processes. How do you generate customer demand? How are products sold? How do your customers use your products? How do you provide after-sales support? This comprehensive trace of your marketing, selling, and servicing processes allows you to create a simple touchpoint map that defines your customers' experiences with your brand.

3. Determine the most influential touchpoints

All touchpoints are not created equal. Some will naturally play a larger role in determining your company's overall customer experience. For example, if your product is ice cream, taste is typically more important than package design. Both are touchpoints, but each has a different effect on our customers' experiences as a whole.

To determine the touchpoints driving your customers' overall experience, your organisation can use a wide array of techniques ranging from quantitative research to institutional knowledge. The methods you use will depend on the complexity of your products, commercial processes, and your existing knowledge base.

4. Design the optimal experience

Once you have completed the above three steps to

building a brand, you should be able to design your optimal customer experience. Determine how to express each reason-to-believe at each key touchpoint. For example, how can you reinforce sporty performance (a reason-to-believe) in product design, at the dealership, and in marketing campaigns?

5. Align the organisation to consistently deliver the optimal experience

A holistic approach to aligning your organisation to consistently deliver the optimal experience is essential. Identify the people, processes, and tools that drive each key touchpoint.

Look beyond employees that have direct contact with your customers. The impacts of behind-the-scenes employees are less obvious but no less important. Similarly, the impact of workflow processes and tools (i.e. technology systems) on the customer experience may be less intuitive but crucial to consistent delivery.

Identify which activities don't align with your envisioned customer experience. Determine how to address them so that these components can be brought into alignment.

Importance of A Business Logo

Business logos aren't just for multi-national corporations! They're for any business that wants to present a professional image and work on establishing customer recognition (otherwise known as branding).

Your logo works for you on your business cards, your business stationery, your invoices and receipts, your business' publications, and, of course, your advertising. Put it on your business' signage, on your yellow pages ad, and on the side of your business' vehicle.

If you have a web site, your business logo should be on every page of your site. Many business people also feature their business logos on any promotional materials they hand out, such as mugs, calendars, and key chains.

The purpose of all this business logo reproduction is to separate your business from the common herd of competitors and build brand recognition and preference.

A good business logo helps your customers remember your business and many people remember images better than they remember words.

Business logo design is fairly simple with all the graphics software programs available, and if you don't have the time or inclination to do it yourself, there are many graphics designers who would love to do this for you. If you're in the process of designing a logo or having one designed remember:

A business logo has to be simple. Simplicity of business logo design makes a logo easy to reproduce and makes it easier for customers to remember and recognise. Limit the number of colours in your business logo, and stay away from muddy colours or tone on tone designs. Think clear contrast and simple shapes when thinking of business logo design.

Your business logo has to have some relevance to your business. For instance, a Christmas tree shape with a bolt of lightning striking it won't be an effective business logo for a computer consulting business. The "picture" the logo represents just doesn't have any association with computers.

It's no coincidence that so many business logos are the initials of the business' name encased in a simple shape; relevant pictorial associations are hard to come by for many businesses, and a symbol that misleads will do more harm than good.

Colours are powerful. Different colours have different associations and can present powerful messages in themselves. Red, as we all know, is seen as fiery and energetic. But what about brown? No matter how much you like a particular shade, it may not be a good choice for your business logo design.

Your business logo has to be scaleable to suit all your promotional needs. The logo you choose has to look good on a business card, on a brochure, and on the side of a bus, for instance, if that's how you choose to advertise. Complicated business logo designs don't scale well.

So keep your business logo design simple, and test how well your logo scales before you rush it into print and get your logo working for you.

Branding Through Your Employees

Your employees are one of the most critical touch points for your customer. Here are several steps to ensure that they are representing your brand in the best light possible.

Develop a Company Philosophy

A thoughtfully planned philosophy that guides how your company operates is the first step to reinforcing your brand among your workforce. In USA, the prestigious Ritz Carlton Hotel Company is an excellent example. They have created the following five "Gold Standards" for their business operations that reinforce the brand and detail an employee's role in delivering on this brand.

A vision to revolutionise hospitality by creating a luxury setting for guests and a credo that states the company's commitment to the genuine care and comfort of its guests.

Three steps of service

— A warm and sincere greeting that uses the guest name, if and when possible;

— Anticipation and compliance with guest needs;

— A fond farewell that uses a guest's name, if and when possible.

7

IMPROVING YOUR SELLING SKILLS

Selling is the art of closing the deal. This definition of selling encapsulates the heart of the matter, because selling is first and foremost a transaction between the seller and the prospective buyer or buyers.

If you're interested in improving your selling skills, you'll find that there are supposedly many kinds of selling that you should use or should avoid, such as high-pressure selling, persuasive selling, no-pressure selling, targeted selling, etc., but all of them amount to the same thing in the end; selling is the art of persuading the consumer that buying the product or service will benefit him or her. Whatever product or service you're selling, then, you need to focus your selling efforts on communicating the benefits of your product or service to the consumer. The benefits may be tangible or intangible, but unless the individual consumer is convinced that he or she will personally experience the benefits, your product or service won't sell.

DEVELOPMENT OF SALES STRATEGY

In today's economy, big and small businesses are seeking

every opportunity to win sales through competitive advantages. Smart owners of small business know a sales strategy can create a competitive advantage.

Selling consists of two main functions: tactics and strategy. Sales strategy is the planning of sales activities: methods of reaching clients, competitive differences and resources available. Tactics involves the day-to-day selling: prospecting, sales process, and follow-up.

The tactics of selling are very important but equally vital is the strategy of sales. The advantages are too compelling to ignore.

Advantages of Sales Planning

— Increased closing ratio by knowing clients hot buttons

— Improved client loyalty by understanding needs

— Shorten the sales cycle with outside recommendations

— Outsell competitors by offering the best solution

Triple-tiered Sales Strategy

The development of any type of plan begins with research.

The insight gained for a competitive advantage comes from the marketplace not from your mind. Look at your client and the outside influences on their business. Approach all three tiers to understand your customer.

Tier 1: Associations: What associations does your target customer belong to? Contact the membership director and establish a relationship not for selling but to understand their member's needs.

Tier 2: Suppliers: Identify non-competitive suppliers who sell to your customer. Learn their challenges and look for partnering solutions.

Tier 3: Customer: Work directly with your customer and ask them what their needs are and if your business may offer a possible solution.

An excellent example of developing a "triple-tiered sales strategy" is a story of a small accounting firm. This firm decided to target independent truck drivers for accounting services. The competition for this firm was a big accounting company. This small business approached the truck drivers association and learned that one concern of their membership was receiving financing for a new vehicle.

A discussion with the suppliers of trucks, revealed financing was only approved after the truckers supplied financial statements. The financials were often prepared by a large accounting firm who set appointments on their time and in their office. The pieces of the puzzle were now coming together. The customer was the last piece of critical information. Truckers were frustrated by the inconvenience of visiting an accounting firm because of the time they spend on the road. The best solution was to bring the accounting service to the customer on their terms and time.

The small accounting office had defined a clear sales strategy: offer in-home financial statement preparation for truck drivers seeking financing through truck manufacturers. All sales leads would be referred from the supplier. This strategy was a win-win for the association, the supplier, the customer and the accounting firm. The moral of the story is to gain a competitive advantage by looking at both sides of the equation, tactics and strategy. Use the triple-tiered approach to win business and outsell the big companies in your market.

Qualifying—Critical Selling Skill

Selling is not a favourite task for many entrepreneurs and small business owners. We picture sales people as greedy, unethical, unscrupulous individuals who are determined to close a sale at any cost. Yet we cannot survive without generating sales so selling skills are a critical competency we need to acquire.

Selling is an honourable profession and everyone who operates a business should learn some fundamentals. From my perspective as a small business owner, sales trainer and consumer, the most important selling skill to learn is how to effectively qualify your prospect.

The most common mistake sales people make is to immediately launch into a product presentation or "pitch" when they first meet their prospect. They extol the virtues of what they sell and tell the prospective buyer how good, fast, reliable, inexpensive or easy to use their product is.

They talk, talk and talk hoping they'll convince the buyer that their product is of value. The problem with this approach is that the "pitch" seldom addresses the issues or concerns of the buyer. Because their needs have not been addressed, there is no compelling reason for them to consider using your machines or to change vendors. If you really want to give prospects a reason to buy from you, you need to give them a reason. One of the most effective ways to do this is to ask a few well thought-out questions to uncover what is important to the prospect. Here are a few examples:

— "I notice you currently use XYZ Vending. How long have they been your supplier?"

— "What do you like most about them?"

— "If you could change one aspect about your current arrangement, what would it be?"

— "What are the most important issues for you?"

— "What have your experiences been with ABC Vending?"

— "How many... .do you sell in an average week/ month?"

— "Who is your primary customer?"

— "Where have you had the most success with your machine(s)?"

Notice that each of these is an open-ended question which means it begins with "who", "what", "where", "why", "when" or "how." These types of questions encourage the prospect to open up and share information of what their needs and wants are. An important note here is to be cautious you don't inadvertently turn these open questions in to closed ones by saying something like; "What are the most important issues for you? Timeliness of service? Income?"

This is a very common mistake that now gives the prospect an answer. But selling is hard enough without making it even more difficult. Never assume you know how they are going to answer. Ask your question and wait patiently for the answer. Even if you have been in the industry for ten years or longer and think you've heard it all, don't make the mistake of assuming you know what the prospect's needs are. Let them tell you, rather than you telling them.

Most people love to talk about themselves and want to share information about their current situation, their challenges or problems, likes and dislikes. But, in most cases, they need prompting. This prompting comes from you in the form of asking the right questions in the proper tone and manner. If you really want to begin differentiating yourself from your competitors take the time to learn about your prospect's situation. By doing so, you'll begin to give them a reason to do business with you instead of someone else.

Methods of Sales Forecasting

Accurate multiple methods

> Sales forecasting is especially difficult when you don't have any previous sales history to guide you, as is the case when you're working on *preparing cash flow projections* as part of writing a business plan. Here, Terry Elliott provides a detailed explanation of how to do sales forecasting. –Ed.

There are all sorts of ways to estimate sales revenues for the purposes of sales forecasting.

One point to remember when sales forecasting is that if you plan to work with a bank for financing, you will want to do multiple estimates so as to have more confidence in the sales forecast. How do you do this?

Sales forecasting method 1

For your type of business, what is the average sales volume per square foot for similar stores in similar locations and similar size? This isn't the final answer for adequate sales forecasting, since a new business won't hit that target for perhaps a year.

But this approach is far more scientific than a general 2 percent figure based on household incomes.

Sales forecasting method 2

For your specific location, how many households needing your goods live within say, one mile? How much will they spend on these items annually, and what percentage of their spending will you get, compared to competitors? Do the same for within five miles (with lower sales forecast figures). (Use distances that make sense for your location.)

Sales forecasting method 3

If you offer say, three types of goods plus two types of extra cost services, estimate sales revenues for each of the five product/service lines. Make an estimate of where you think you'll be in six months (such as "we should be selling five of these items a day, plus three of these, plus two of these.") and calculate the gross sales per day. Then multiply by 30 for the month.

Now scale proportionately from month one to month six; that is, build up from no sales (or few sales) to your six month sales level. Now carry it out from months six through 12 for a complete annual sales forecast.

Don't just do one sales forecast

Instead of forecasting annual sales as a single figure, use one or two of the sales forecasting methods above and generate three figures: pessimistic, optimistic, and realistic. Then put the figures in by month, as depending on your business, there could be huge variations by month.

Expenses in Sales Forecasting

Now put in your expenses by month, including big purchases by season (or however you buy materials/ goods). Remember, you may buy materials or inventory in say, July, for Diwali, yet not get all of your receipts until 25 days after Diwali. There can be big cash flow implications. Also, will you be buying vehicles? Capital equipment? Make sure to show depreciation expense.

In your expenses, put in an allowance for bad debts. Figure how much of your sales are by cash, how much by credit card, how much by your extending credit. Deduct say four percent or more for credit card expense for that portion sold by credit card. For payroll expenses, put in estimated tax withholding payments quarterly that must be paid to the government.

If you're going to a bank for financing, be able to answer questions such as, have you made an allowance for a reserve cash account, for your slow months, but also in case you have to quickly replace a vehicle or equipment? You say you'll charge x rupees for your product, but what happens when your competition cuts the price by 33 percent and still makes a profit?

How specifically will you grow your business—selling more to existing customers, selling existing products to new customers, selling new products to existing customers, and selling new products in order to attract new customers? They're going to want to see if you've got a real plan. Remember that it is acceptable (and realistic) to have a negative cash flow projection for the early months of your cash flow projection period.

Selling Self-confidence

Small business success programme

To sell, you must believe in your product or service - and believe in yourself. Your selling skills depend, in large part, on your level of self-confidence. Other people sense whether or not you believe in yourself, and by extension, whether or not you believe in what you're doing. That belief is what persuades the customer or client to buy the product or service. Therefore, increasing your self-confidence will improve your selling skills.

Cultivate self-confidence

Do you believe that you personally are not good at selling? Are worry and anxiety eroding your self confidence? Everyone has these feelings at one time or another. But that doesn't mean that you can't sell successfully. Believing in yourself is like any other attitude; self-confidence can be learned. You can increase your self-confidence through practice, and that in turn will increase your selling skills.

Using self-praise

We are surrounded by negative influences. But most of these negative influences exist in our own heads. Awake or asleep, our minds constantly produce a series of thoughts and images, and for many of us, these produce a constant barrage of negative messages.

Using self-praise is a self-confidence building technique for combating these negative messages. Instead of allowing your mind to produce whatever messages it wants, consciously override these messages with positive praise about what you've done or do well. For instance, say to yourself, "You really handled that crisis well yesterday, when you..." , or "You're really great at...". Your self-confidence will bloom more readily in a positive mental climate.

Tips to Building Self-confidence Routine

Like the daily planning session, your building self-confidence routine needs to be uninterrupted. Do not take phone calls during this time, or let family members interrupt you.

It helps to physically confront yourself when you're conducting a self-praise session to build your self-confidence. Many people find it helpful to stand in front of a mirror when they're doing this, and to speak out loud. Once you've become comfortable with the technique, you may wish to go through the self-praise exercise mentally, and combine it with other activities, such as exercise or household tasks.

If you haven't used a self-confidence building technique such as self-praise at first, you'll probably feel silly when you first start. Ignore these feelings and persevere. Over time, you'll find your feelings of silliness diminish as your self confidence grows. The more specific you make your self-praise, the more powerful it will be. And the more you use your building self-confidence routine, the more your internal self-confidence will develop—the self-confidence you need to sell your product or service successfully.

Self-confidence and Sales Related Reading

— Visualise success

— Qualifying - the critical selling skill

— Cold calling tips

Homework assignment

Develop a personal building self-confidence routine and use it every day this week.

Your building self-confidence routine may be as simple as using a five minute session of self-praise each day, or as complex as using several techniques such as visualising success and self-praise with whatever elements of your personal routine you find work best for you.

Many people find that going through their building self-confidence routine just before their daily business planning session gives their day a positive energy that helps them be more productive throughout the day.

Steps to Increase Sales

Shift your sales focus for increased sales

Want to increase sales dramatically? Then shift your sales focus from attracting new customers to enticing your proven customers to buy again. The best sales prospect is a prospect that's already converted – in other words, one of your current customers.

Think of it this way; if your business is located in a small town with a population of 1000 people and you sell a sprocket to everyone in that town, man, woman, and child, you've sold 1000 sprockets – and saturated your market. Your sprocket selling days are over. Is it time to pack up and move on?

Try some or all of these ideas to increase your sales:

1. Set up a sales incentive programme

Give your sales staff a reason to get out there and sell, sell, sell. Why do so many businesses that rely on their sales staff to drive sales have incentive programmes in place? Because offering their sales staff the trips and/or TVs for x amount of sales works.

2. Encourage your sales staff to upsell

Essentially, upselling involves adding related products and/or services to your line and making it convenient and necessary for customer to buy them. Just placing more products near your usual products isn't going to increase your sales much. To upsell successfully, the customer has to be persuaded of the benefit.

3. Give your customers the inside scoop

If you have a promotion or sale coming up, tell your customers about it. They'll come back – and probably bring some friends with them too.

4. Tier your customers

There should be a clear and obvious difference between regular customers and other customers – a difference that your regular customers perceive as showing that you value them. How can you expect customer loyalty if all customers are treated as "someone off the street"? There are all kinds of ways that you can show your regular customers that you value them, from small things such as greeting them by name through larger benefits such as giving regulars extended credit or discounts.

5. Set up a customer rewards programme

We're all familiar with the customer rewards programmes that so many large businesses have in place. But there's no reason that a small business can't have a customer rewards programme, too. It can be as simple as a discount on a customer's birthday or as complex as a points system that earns various rewards such as discounts on merchandise. Done right, rewards programmes can really help build customer loyalty and increase sales.

6. Distribute free samples to customers

Why do so many businesses include free samples of other

products when you buy something from them? Because it can increase sales in so many ways. At the very least, the original customer will be thinking warm thoughts about your company, and hopefully telling other people about your products.

Attracting new customers is a good thing. But attracting new customers is not the only way to increase your sales, and is, in fact, the hard way of going about it. Shifting your sales focus to enticing your current customers can make increasing your sales easier – and best of all, build the customer loyalty that results in repeat sales.

Sales Blunders

Avoiding the mistakes

We all make mistakes when selling our product or service. Here are the most common sales mistakes people make.

Sales mistake 1: Allowing a prospect to lead the sales process. The best way to control the sales interaction is to ask questions. This is also the best way to learn whether or not your product or service meets the needs of your prospect. Quality questions that uncover specific issues, problems, or corporate objectives are essential in helping you establish yourself as an expert.

Sales mistake 2: Not completing pre-meeting research. This approach is one of most common sales mistakes. Invest the time learning about your prospect before you call them and before you try to schedule a meeting.

Sales mistake 3: Talking too much. Too many sales people talk too much during the sales interaction. They espouse about their product, its features, their service and so on.

Sales mistake 4: Giving the prospect information that is irrelevant.

Sales mistake 5: Not being prepared. You have exactly one opportunity to make a great first impression and you will not make it if you are not prepared.

Sales mistake 6: Neglecting to ask for the sale. If you sell a product or service, you have the obligation to ask the customer for a commitment, particularly if you have invested time assessing their needs and know that your product or service will solve a problem. Many people are concerned with coming across as pushy but as long as you ask for the sale in a non-threatening, confident manner, people will usually respond favourably.

Sales mistake 7: Failing to prospect. This is one of the most common mistakes independent business make. When business is good many people stop prospecting, thinking that the flow of business will continue. However, the most successful sales people prospect all the time. They schedule prospecting time in their agenda every week.

Even the most seasoned sales professional makes mistakes from time to time. Avoid these blunders and increase the likelihood of closing the sale.

Increasing Sales in Existing Markets

Growth strategy

Increasing sales in an existing market is one of the easiest ways to grow your business. You already have a head start with this growth strategy as once your business is established, it has regular customers, and, like all businesses, you've collected all kinds of information about them. The key to successfully increasing your sales in an existing market is to know your customers' buying histories, both generally and individually.

The goal, of course, is to get your existing customers to buy more. The data about what your customers buy, when and how often will help you make savvy decisions about stocking and marketing. Cold drinks a hot seller in the summer? Offer a bulk buy discount. Or use your hot sellers to move other items that aren't doing as well. When they buy the hot item, give them the opportunity to buy another related item at a reduced price.

Looking for a shortcut for implementing this growth strategy? Institute a frequent buyers reward programme. Such a programme doesn't need to be complicated. One way to do this is simply to offer your regular customers a straight discount on whatever they buy, such as 10 percent.

Another approach is to tie the discount to purchasing a specific amount, such as offering 10 percent off for every two thousand rupees a customer spends. Yet another approach to this growth strategy for increasing sales in an existing market is to offer other merchandise as rewards to frequent buyers. The key to success with any frequent buyers reward programme is to make sure the rules are clear and applied equitably.

Bulk buys, purchase incentives, and frequent buyer reward programmes are all examples of business growth strategies for increasing sales in existing markets based on the general buying histories of your customers. Business growth strategies based on individual customer buying histories can be even more powerful. An individual customer's buying history gives you insight into her preferences and attitudes and allows you to customise your sales and marketing efforts.

You see, if done right, customised sales and marketing efforts build customer loyalty – which also helps to increase sales. Websites are ideal for this kind of customised sales effort.

8

INTERNET MARKETING STRATEGIES

Internet marketing means different things to different people. Essentially, though, Internet marketing refers to the strategies that are used to market a product or service online, marketing strategies that include search engine optimisation and search engine submission, copywriting that encourages site visitors to take action, web site design strategies, online promotions, reciprocal linking, and email marketing—and that's just hitting the highlights.

Online marketers are constantly devising new Internet marketing strategies in the hopes of driving more traffic to their Web sites and making more sales; witness the increasing use of blogs as marketing tools for business, for instance. Depending on whom you ask, the term *Internet marketing* can mean a variety of things. At one time, Internet marketing consisted mostly of having a website or placing banner ads on other websites. On the other end of the spectrum, there are loads of companies telling you that you can make a fortune overnight on the Internet and who try to sell you some form of "Internet marketing program".

Today, Internet marketing is evolving into a broader mix of components a company can use as a means of increasing sales - even if your business is done completely online, partly online, or completely offline. The decision to use Internet marketing as part of a company's overall marketing strategy is strictly up to the company of course, but as a rule, Internet marketing is becoming an increasingly important part of nearly every company's marketing mix.

For some online businesses, it is the only form of marketing being practiced.

OBJECTIVES OF INTERNET MARKETING

Essentially, Internet marketing is using the Internet to do one or more of the following:

— Communicate a company's message about itself, its products, or its services.

— Conduct research as to the nature (demographics, preferences, and needs) of existing and potential customers.

— Sell goods, services, or advertising space over the Internet.

COMPONENTS OF INTERNET MARKETING

Components of Internet marketing may include:

— A website, consisting of text, images and possibly audio and video elements used to convey the company's message, to inform existing and potential customers of the features and benefits of the company's products and/or services. The website may or may not include the ability to capture leads on potential customers or directly sell a product or service online. A website can be the offline equivalent of a brochure or a mail order catalog and is a great way to establish your business identity.

— *Search Engine Marketing (SEM),* which is marketing a website via search engines, either by improving the site's natural (organic) ranking through search engine optimisation (SEO), buying pay-per-click (PPC) ads with search engines which are based on selected keywords and then displayed on search engine results pages when those keywords are used in a search, and/or on other websites whose content includes the keywords specified, pay-for-inclusion (PFI) listings in website directories. PFI listings are similar to offline yellow page listings.

— *Email marketing,* which is a method of distributing information about a product or service or for soliciting feedback from customers about a product or service through Email. Email addresses of customers and prospective customers may be collected or purchased. Various methods are used, such as the regular distribution of newsletters or mass mailing of offers related to the company's product or services. Email marketing is essentially the online equivalent of direct mail marketing.

— *Banner advertising,* which is the placement of ads on a website for a fee. Offline this would be similar to traditional advertising in newspapers or magazines.

— *Online promotion,* including press release distribution, which involves placing a newsworthy story about a company, its website, its people, and/or its products/services with on online wire service, or blog (web log) activity, which is the act of posting comments, expressing opinions or making announcements in a discussion forum. Blog marketing can be accomplished in blogs either by hosting your own blog or by posting comments and/or URLs in other blogs related to your product or service.

INTERNET MARKETING AND HOME BUSINESS

Of all of the components of Internet marketing, prospective customers and clients expect a business to have a website. In fact, not having one could raise a red flag to a prospect. Online usage has become so pervasive today, many prospects might easily choose to do business with a company that they can get up-to-date information on 24 hours per day, 7 days per week.

Even a business that only has very local customers, such as a single location restaurant or shoe store can benefit from having a Web site. And, those businesses whose customers are not restricted to a geographical area might have a difficult time finding an alternate method of attracting customers that offers the reasonably low expense and worldwide reach of a Web presence.

Because of the "virtual" nature of most home businesses, websites, if not an absolute necessity, can certainly provide benefits to a home business operator. Since most home-based businesses don't have a physical location, a website provides an inexpensive means for prospects to get to know what you do or what you sell and can even be a "storefront" for selling goods and services directly. The Internet has greatly enabled home businesses to prosper because of the reasonably low cost to start and maintain a web presence. Therefore, Internet marketing should be part of your business plan and your marketing strategy.

Internet Marketing Mix

How much of your marketing strategy should be handled

online, which Internet marketing elements you use, and the importance you should give to your Web site, depends on the nature of your business, your budget, and, to some extent, your personal traits.

Unless you transact business only online, for example if you are an eBay reseller, you will probably want to include some traditional offline marketing elements in your strategy. Even those who conduct business only online might consider placing traditional ads in newspapers or magazines to bring prospects to their website to transact business. Perfect examples of this are Expedia, Travelocity and Monster.com. While they are online businesses, they invest heavily in traditional advertising, including radio and TV advertising, to draw traffic to their sites where the actual business is conducted.

If you have a personal distaste for "spam", which most of us do, you may not want to include Email marketing in your Internet marketing strategy. However, Email marketing doesn't have to mean just sending out unsolicited messages to every email address you can gather. If you include a visitor registration form on your website, for example, or if you exhibit at trade shows, you have the vehicles needed to collect email addresses of interested prospects. You might consider creating a newsletter and sending it to these prospects on a regular basis. Or, you might just set up a schedule where you periodically send an email to your interested prospects to see how they're doing, if you can be of assistance to them, or if their needs have changed since you last talked.

Of course, your budget will also determine the components you use in your Internet marketing strategy. A website will require you to register a domain name and to purchase web hosting services for your website.

Once that's done, you'll need a design and content for your website, which you'll either need to provide yourself or pay to have a web content professional and/ or web designer handle it for you.

Once your content and design are in place, you'll want your site to be found, so you'll want to either learn about search engine optimisation (SEO) or pay an SEO contractor to do it for you. Depending on your budget, you should also research which directories are available and how much they cost for a paid listing (PFI).

Ideally, if you pay to have web content written for you, that content should be optimised when it's written. Likewise, you or your web designer should know something about SEO because how your site is designed can enhance or limit your site traffic. In both cases, you may pay a bit more, but you'll save time in the long run. Once the site is up and running, you'll either need to maintain it yourself or outsource the duties to an independent Webmaster to do it for you.

Pay-per-click advertising, like Google AdWords can be easy on your budget because you can specify how much you're willing to pay when someone clicks your ad and how much you're willing to pay per day. You can also specify whether you want to include your ad only on search pages or on other websites related to your keywords. Plus, they're fairly easy to activate, disable, rack, and update. You can also use images with PPC advertising, which may be more cost effective than placing banner ads on other Web sites.

On the other side of the coin, you can use pay per click ads to make money with your website, through programs like *Google AdSense,* Yahoo Publisher or Microsoft AdCenter.

Tracking Results

Let's face it: the average home business operator is not awash in cash. If you're going to be spending money on Internet marketing you need to track its effectiveness. As you do so, you'll discover what works and what doesn't work for your business. And, you can learn from the mistakes you make in your Internet advertising campaign to become an Internet advertising success. Knowing what's worth spending money on and what isn't is critical for your business success.

Keep in mind, in most cases patience is a true virtue. Search engines aren't likely to find you overnight and your Internet marketing campaign and search engine marketing programs may not generate a bundle of revenue right away. Because you'll have literally millions of competitors on the Internet, it will behoove you to keep up to date and keep on your toes. However, some knowledge, some capable assistance, and a well-managed Internet marketing strategy can increase your chances for home business success.

INTERNET MARKETING AND PROFESSIONAL SERVICES

There's more marketing hype published on the Internet in one day than P.T. Barnum generated in his lifetime. Like a worm swallowing its tail, the Internet marketing beast feeds mostly on itself. The vast majority of what appears on the Internet about marketing is designed to help you market products and services sold and delivered exclusively on the Internet.

So what does that mean for the independent professional whose web presence is primarily aimed at selling his or her own personal services? You know, services delivered the old-fashioned way, by humans interacting face-to-face or at least voice-to-voice. At best, the average professional is likely to be overwhelmed by the sheer volume of Internet marketing advice available. At worst, he or she is being seriously misled by it.

The problem is that marketing your own professional services is simply not the same as marketing a retail product or an anonymous business service. You can't sell corporate consulting like you do web hosting; nor can you sell life coaching the same way you do an e-book. If you try to market yourself by following advice designed for marketing Internet products and services, you're likely to make some serious mistakes.

Internet Marketing Myths

Here are five Internet marketing myths that may be hazardous to the health of your business.

It all starts with a great website

Actually, the place where it starts is with a well-defined service. If you don't have a crystal clear picture of who you are marketing to and exactly what you're selling them, the best website in the world won't get you clients. Before you even think about building a website, you should know who your target market is, how to describe your professional specialty, and what specific benefits your work provides for your clients.

The content of your site is much more important than the design. Yes, you should have a professional-looking site, but a brilliant design and dazzling graphics won't pay off anywhere near as well as a clear explanation of why a client should work with you. Useful material such as articles, assessments, and other samples of your expertise will go much further to persuade prospective clients than flash intros and interactive menus.

More traffic translates to increased profits

The only result that more traffic to your website guarantees you is increased bandwidth use by your web host. Before spending money on banner ads, web directories, or pay-per-click listings to drive more visitors to your site, you need to be sure that they'll want to do business with you once they get there.

Ask your colleagues and current clients to critique your site. Do they understand what you are offering? Can they see concrete benefits to your target audience? Revise your site based on their feedback. Then personally invite some prospective clients to visit and touch base afterward. Do your prospects seem more inclined to do business with you after seeing your site? If so, you're on the right track. If not, you still have more work to do.

Do whatever it takes to build your list

There's no question that a substantial opt-in mailing list is a valuable marketing asset, but the quality of names on your list is much more important than the quantity. Acquiring names through giveaways of other people's material, trading lists with joint venture partners, or purchasing them from a vendor rarely provides qualified buyers truly interested in your services.

Absolutely, ask your site visitors and people you meet to join your mailing list and offer them something of value in return. A well-written ezine, helpful report, or informative audio are all effective premiums. But, your premium should be directly related to the services you provide and also serve to increase your professional credibility. Names acquired from promotional gimmicks or unknown sources seldom turn into paying clients.

Killer copy is the secret to sales

Hype-laden web copy may be effective in selling certain info-products or courses, but it hardly inspires trust. You're not going to convince anyone to hire you individually as a consultant, coach, trainer, designer, or financial advisor by offering "not one, not two, but three valuable bonuses" as if you were selling steak knives on late-night TV.

Your Internet marketing persona should reflect the same professionalism as the work you do with your clients.

If writing marketing materials isn't your forte, by all means hire a professional copywriter. But be sure you hire one with experience writing for professionals like yourself. The copy on your website should inspire feelings of confidence about your abilities, and communicate your reliability and solid qualifications.

Just follow the winning formula and you will get rich

There's only one surefire recipe for Internet wealth, that's the business of selling surefire recipes. There seems to be an infinite number of buyers for every new get-rich-on-the-net scheme that is invented, but paradoxically, a precious few people actually making money on the web.

The Internet may be a different medium for marketing professional services than making calls, writing letters, or speaking to people in person, but the same time-honored principles still apply. There is no new winning formula. The secret to landing clients is what it always has been — build relationships and get people to know, like, and trust you.

If your website, ezine, and other Internet-based activities contribute to building long-term, trusting relationships with prospective clients and referral sources, you'll get business on the web. But if you blast your message out to anyone who will listen, aiming for a quick profit, the Internet won't bring you any more business than standing on a street corner with a megaphone.

Free Web Site Promotion Techniques

The thing to remember about free Web site promotion is that nothing is ever truly free. If you don't spend money promoting your Web site, you're going to have to spend time. So why waste time on Web site promotion methods that will only bring you minuscule returns, if any? If you're prepared to work on them, these five free Web site promotion techniques will deliver, rewarding you with increased site traffic.

1. Work on SEO

SEO stands for Search Engine Optimisation and it's the best thing since sliced bread in terms of free Web site promotion. Search Engine Optimisation is the process of making Web site pages attractive to search engines, and the great thing is that it's not hard to learn and apply the basics to your own Web site(s). Through working on SEO, you can improve the page rankings of your Web pages and drive more traffic to your site.

2. Get others to link to you

When other people put a link to your site on their site, you get free web site promotion. You also get a shot at a better search engine ranking for your page. All of the big three search engines (Google, Yahoo, and MSN) use inbound links as an important part of the formula that determines a page's rank.

Be aware though that it's not just a numbers game; it's the quality of the links that really matters. So you want to focus your reciprocal linking efforts on relevant quality links. The standard procedure is to search for and identify relevant sites that you would like to have link to yours and then send their webmasters email requesting a link on their site, offering a link on your site in return.

Tip: You can check a Web site or Web page's ranking before you try to reciprocally link with it by using SEO tools such as *Page Rank Lookup* and the *Link Popularity Tool. Google's Toolbar* also has a Page Rank Display feature. These tools are also handy for checking the status and progress of your own Web site and/or pages.

3. Write articles

The beauty of this free Web site promotion strategy is that once again someone else is promoting your Web site for you. And if you get your articles published on popular, long-lived Web sites or in well-known magazines, they can be sitting there promoting your Web site for a long, long time with no further effort on your part.

However, there are catches. First, you have to be able to write well on a topic or topics that other people will want to read and/or publish. Second, you have to find the quality places for your articles to be published and persuade the people making the decisions to publish them. When you find them, send an email asking if they can use a particular piece, including your article so they can look at it right away if they're interested. Be sure your email mentions that they are welcome to publish the piece for free. Also be sure that your piece ends with a "resource box" or "blurb" that promotes you and your Web site.

Tip: Find the Web sites or magazines you want to be published on first, and then spend some time reading the content to see what type of material they might want and if there are any obvious holes in their content that you could cover. Then tailor your material to that particular site or magazine's needs.

Building a Business Web Site

Promoting your business web site was a very easy process. You placed 3 lines of code called "meta tags" on the top of your home page and submitted the page to free search engines or directories. Fast forward to the present. Web site promotion has become a time consuming project and a new position in the web design industry, Search Engine Consultants, has been created. Use the list below to find ways that your business web site will be found by your ideal client, is user friendly and is visited often.

1. Build a strong, solid business foundation. Design a business plan, marketing plan, ideal client profile and 30-second elevator speech.
2. Be consistent and "brand" your company. Use the same colors, logo, motto, etc. everywhere on your business web site!
3. Make your business web site trustable.
4. Create policies that build trust: customer service, code of ethics and newsletter privacy policy.
5. Ask your web master to name each of your pages using a keyword you have supplied them with.
6. Offer added values on your business web site that make sense to your business and ideal client. This can include affiliate programs, books, and recommended links to web sites.
7. Add a "favourites or bookmark this site" script to some of your business web site pages.

8. Add a "Recommend This Site" on your site. If someone visits your business Web site and knows someone else who may appreciate it, this feature will e-mail the page's link to a recipient.
9. If you have pages on your business web site that you update monthly (like an articles page or recommended links page) say so on the page.
10. Join a few Web rings. For additional information, visit WebRing and Bravenet.
11. Provide a subscription box, to your e-zine or business announcement list, on your most viewed business web site pages.
12. On large business web sites, create a "What's New Page" or even better, ask your web designer to design a "Site Map" for your visitors.

Search engine submission tips

Much of your business web site traffic will come from search engines. Here are some search engine submission tips to keep in mind.

13. Search engines look for certain things - titles, headings, meta tags - so it is crucial to make sure your site is "search engine friendly". Visit the Search Engine Optimisation and Submission page on this site for additional resources on search engines and search engine submission tips.
   (*a*). *Title tags:* Title tags should be 60 or so characters and include some keywords.
   (*b*). *Header tags are numbered from 1 to 7:* some search engines recognise Header tags. So make sure you use these tags for each of the titles on your page.

(*c*). *Keyword Meta tags:* Add no more than 15 to 20 keywords to keep the search engines from flagging your site for keyword spamming.

Prioritise your words. The best way to submit to search engines is to submit to each search engine individually.

(*d*) Use keywords in the text area of each page. They are especially important at the beginning of sentences and higher up on the page.

(*e*) To learn more about meta tags and choosing keywords, read *"Effective Search Engine Optimisation"*.

14. Search engines do not find your site unless you submit your site's information to them. Below are four ways to submit your Web site to search engines:

(*a*) It is recommended that you submit to search engines individually.

(*b*) Since some people prefer to use a free service to submit their sites to search engines, they open a free e-mail address to use when you do "anything" for free on the World Wide Web. Two good search engine submission services are *Submit It!,* and *Scrub The Web.* You can pay for a program that will assist you to submit and critique your site such as *WebPosition Gold.*

(*c*) Hire a Search Engine Optimisation Expert to handle your search engine submissions.

15 Visit these search engine information sites: Search Engine Watch and Search Engine Guide.

Web site promotion tips

Making sure your business web site is search engine

friendly is only one aspect of Web site promotion. Here are some other web site promotion tips:

16. Find easy and secure ways for your clients to pay you. A shopping cart and a secure way to accept checks and/or credit cards work very well.
17. Check your business web site's links regularly to make sure they all work. Use a free link checker such as Xenu's Link Sleuth.
18. Provide monthly chats or bulletin boards (forums) to build relationships and community.
19. Conduct periodic contests and announce the winners on your site.
20. Offer a free e-book or e-report on your site. Its size doesn't matter if you're providing it for free and it's specifically for your ideal client.

    Provide permission for the e-book to be forwarded to others for their personal use.
21. Write articles, post them to your business Web site, and submit them to *article banks.*
22. Design some quizzes or surveys. Statistics show that visitors love quizzes and assessment tools.
23. Participate in online forums as an expert. You get to "quietly" promote your business in your three or four line signature.
24. Place your business web site address on all your printed literature — business cards, brochures, newsletters, letterhead, e-mail signature, ads - everything!!
25. Promote your web address in your signature for e-mails (change it regularly to highlight something new you're promoting).
26. Teach classes or speak to groups about subjects relating to your products.

27. Network locally to bring people to your site.
28. "Permission Market" by gathering, in writing, the e-mail addresses of students, or an audience as part of your evaluation forms. Create index cards so that you can invite your friends, networking partners or associates to join your list. Keep any papers involved in this process for at least a year or two.
29. When your business web site is launched, updated, or you write a free e-book, send a Press Release to the media, your clients, and friends and associates, too.
30. Want to know more about Internet Marketing? Visit this *Internet Marketing Index* at Internet.com's Interactive Marketing Channel.
31. If this list of web site promotion ideas seems overwhelming, visit your favourite search engine to conduct a search for Search Engine Optimisers and Consultants or ask others who they use and would recommend.

LEVELS OF INTERNET MARKETING AND THE SALES PROCESS

You can provide human interaction to potential Internet clients and customers so that you are able to move that client or customer through a successful sales process, but how? You do this by following a five step process in your Internet marketing strategy that continually builds trust and confidence by meeting the psychological marketing needs of that visitor and potential customer while escorting that visitor through the selection and purchasing process.

Creating a successful online sales process can be accomplished by making sure that you represent and court your visitor through the five levels of the sales process on your site.

Anyone who has studied any marketing at all knows that there are psychological needs that must be met in order for a person to be persuaded to purchase a product or service.

If it's a product you are selling are you representing that product to solve a specific problem or meet a specific need? If you are selling a service are you getting in touch with the pain of your potential client to draw their interest into what you are offering?

There are steps that you can take to effectively do that and in response witness the successful sales process over and over in the virtual world that is why an Internet marketing strategy is a necessity not an option.

The five levels of the sales process build on one another in many ways. An Internet Marketing Strategy that is done correctly will clearly define all five levels of the process and how they are represented through your site. The strategy will then assist you in setting realistic and attainable Internet marketing goals. It will also assist you in using each step to build and influence the others so that the process continually moves toward the successful close of the sale.

These five levels of the sales process are the core components that will move your website viewer from visitor to customer or client. By representing each level that is mentioned below and courting your potential client or customer through those levels you will have the power to move your site from failure to success.

— Marketing/Prospecting to your Target Market and Audience

— Build Credibility and Trust - (Your viewer needs this to move forward)

— Escort and Court the Buyer through the Process - (Meet their Needs 7 out of 10 want to buy!)

— Present the Product or Service that meets their needs

— Successfully Close the Sale

Let's explore each phase in depth, so that you have a greater understanding of how you can put these princples to work for your business.

Levels 1, 2, and 3 of the Internet Marketing and Sales Process

Level 1: Marketing/prospecting

Prospecting is the result of your marketing. It's the delivery of targeted qualified traffic to your virtual storefront. This can be achieved by search engine optimisation, pay per clicks, or advertisements that draw people to your site. Once they are there it is your job and responsibility to deliver your Unique Selling Proposition. Not sure what your USP is? Ask yourself the following questions:

— What is the obvious void in the marketplace that your product or service fills?

— What makes your business stand out as distinct and appealing that sets your business apart from the rest?

Level 2: Build Credibility and Trust

In a brick and mortar business trust is built by human interaction. Greeting a person when they walk in the door or physically helping them find something that they are looking for, so how can you build that same trust and credibility virtually?

Your viewer is unconsciously judging your credibility by mentally asking themselves the following questions:

— Does this feel and look professional like a legitimate company?
— Is this site reliable?
— How fast is it downloading and are there broken images or links?
— Can I find my way through the site with the navigation that is provided, or are these virtual isles cluttered?
— How is the copy on this site?
— Is it powerful, does it draw me in or is obvious that there was no time taken to write it?
— Are there spelling and grammatical errors?
— Do the images draw me in or are they distracting and irrelevant?
— Can I find the companies assurances and privacy policies easily?
— What about customer support? Is it easily found?
— Can I access support and information that I need easily or is it hidden?

Take a look at your site and ask yourself the questions above. Are you guiding your viewers or are you leaving them in the dark. Your site should work as a personal shopper, a live virtual assistant that knows the needs that your visitor has and makes the solutions for those needs easily accessible.

Level 3: Escort and Court the Buyer

A person who visits your site has been targeted if you followed the first steps in prospecting, so now it's time to qualify the visitor. How do you do this? It's actually very easy. A person happens on your site because they are looking for a solution to a problem. That solution can be a product or a service. Internet marketing studies show that 7 out of 10 visitors to a site are ready to buy. Take the time to escort and court them to what they need.

— When you look at your current site are you helping your visitors to identify and find the best solution for that problem?

— Are you guiding them to find what they need to solve the problem that they have?

Your navigation should be structured to help those that know exactly what it is that they are looking for, those who know what they want in general but aren't sure about the specifics, and those that are browsing and need you to give them some direction.

Level 4: Present the Product/service

The presentation process is how you are presenting your products or services to your visitors as you guide them through the selection process after you have escorted them and found out what their needs are in the previous stage. It's important to remember that each level ofthe process overlaps. As you present your products or services to your visitor, be sure that you are continually keeping their attention and interest by motivating them to continue with the sale.

Level 5: Close the Sale

Does your site close the sale effectively? Take a look at each product that you offer, are you providing enough information about the product are you giving them assurance policies and/or guarantees regarding their purchase? Are your product descriptions enticing? Does your description answer common questions that visitors might have? Consider adding testimonials for each product or service to build added credibility.

One thing that many e-commerce sites forget to do is provide payment information. Do you take credit cards, if so which ones? Another vital part of the close that is often missed is clearly communicating your guarantee and assurance that you will stand behind the product or service. If you represent each level that is mentioned above and effectively court your potential client or customer through the five levels you will have the power to move your website from failure to success.

9

IDENTIFYING YOUR NICHE MARKET

Niche market is a focused, targetable portion of a market. By definition, then, a business that focuses on a niche market is addressing a need for a product or service that is not being addressed by mainstream providers. You can think of a niche market as a narrowly defined group of potential customers.

For instance, instead of offering cleaning services, a business might establish a niche market by specialising in blind cleaning services. Why should you bother to establish a niche market? Because of the great advantage of being alone there; other small businesses may not be aware of your particular niche market, and large businesses won't want to bother with it. The trick to capitalising on a niche market is to find or develop a market niche that has customers who are accessible, that is growing fast enough, and that is not owned by one established vendor already.

DEFINING NICHE MARKET

Often business owners view a niche market as narrowing their sales or cutting into a profit margin, so they fear it. The truth is a niche market could be defined as a component that gives your business power. A niche market allows you to define who you are marketing to.

When you know who are you are marketing to it's easy to determine where your marketing energy and dollars should be spent. Take for example a car dealership. A car dealership calls me up and tells me they want me to help them develop an Internet Marketing strategy.

There is even a greater importance in having a well-defined niche market when planning your Internet Marketing strategy to achieve Internet Success. The most common misconception about online marketing is that if you build it they will come or having an online business will make you wealthy. Truth is you have to find your niche market to get them to come and you must offer a product or service that they are demanding to reach a level of financial success via the Internet.

Defining your niche market before you embark on your Internet marketing strategy is important for the following 5 reasons.

— You have the ability to maximise your marketing budget by targeting your defined niche market. You'll know exactly where to advertise. You'll know where to look to find ezines and related sites that are catering to your market. This gives you a starting point.

— Your site can then be optimised for search engines so that your niche market can find you easily.

— You are able to cater your site to your niche market.You can develop your site to guide your viewers and help them find solutions or products that you offer that are specific to the problems that your niche market encounters.

— A defined niche market makes it easier to develop ideas for new products or services that inherently appeal to your specific niche.

— You have an upper-hand in establishing yourself as a leader in your industry.

Do you now see the importance of having a niche market? Are you struggling with who your niche market is? If you answered yes spend some time asking yourself the following questions:

— What is it that my current clients have in common?

— How do I set myself apart from the competition?

— What is different about services or products that I offer?

— What are the "extras" that I bring to the market?

The best way to answer these questions is without analysing them too much. Just write down what it is that first comes to mind. Once you've completed them analyse the answer and it will be easy to define your niche market.

TARGETING THE PROSPECTS

Unique Offering and Avoid the Competition

Many entrepreneurs think that selling to the widest possible market is the likeliest path to success. They are afraid to pursue a market niche because they fear they'll lose business by turning away customers. But this 'take all comers' approach is not very effective. It's hard to stand out when you market your business without a distinctive set of prospects in mind.

Occupying a niche means you won't be competing with a lot of similar businesses solely on price. And because you will be selling products and services that are customised to the specific needs and predispositions of a select group of people, you can often charge more. Your products and services serve a market that can't easily find alternatives.

The process starts with market research: analyse your best potential customers, your competitors, your market's predisposition toward your products and services, and your ability to serve these people so well as to make you their vendor of choice.

Market research is like sticking your toe into a lake before jumping in. If you figure out exactly which group of people you want to reach, and what their needs are, you avoid wasting time and money. Once you know, you can alter your product or services to fit the needs of your target market more closely, and you can craft a message that reflects your business and your customer.

Market research does not require expensive consultants, surveys or focus groups— it can be as simple as asking your best customers the right questions. To determine if a particular niche is right for you, ask yourself these questions:

- — Do I have an identifiable target population with similar interests and needs?
- — Is the market large enough to support my business?
- — Can I tailor my products, services, and business identity to address that market's particular needs?
- — Is my target market currently underserved?
- — Can I reach my potential customers in a cost-effective manner?

Your niche will give your marketing efforts a natural, sharp focus. The more you specialise, the more your market will see the value of your services because you speak directly to their unique situation. Assuming your niche is large enough, you can do quite well by becoming a provider of products and services that can't be found anywhere else.

Larry Klein discovered his target market from the inside. A successful financial advisor, he retired from his primary job and became a marketing guru to other financial professionals. He knew they needed marketing help, but as he talked to them and worked with them, he discovered that what they wanted most were ways to reach seniors.

Klein explains, "I'm not 60. So, you don't have to be a member of your ideal marketplace. But if you talk to enough people in that market group, you're going to get it. You have to be awake and aware and be listening for what it is."

All the information you need to target and succeed in an ideal marketplace is out there waiting to be found," says Klein. "You can take the guesswork out of building a business."

Having talked to enough seniors to understand their needs, Klein refined a series of methods for approaching them with investment opportunities. Now he offers seminars and writes articles about these strategies and has defined himself as a specialist in this area.

NICHE MARKETING VS. MASS MARKETING

Visualise the mass marketing person as standing smack in the middle of a major league park. On the ground, in front of this person, is a large pile of various denominations of currency. The mass marketing person just set this pile of currency on fire. He wants to attract the attention of the seated spectators using the smoke from the burning currency. He has put out the word that smoke from burning currency will clear all eight sinus cavities.

Since the ballpark is so huge, by the time the smoke reaches the park's perimeter, it will be severely diluted by the size of the park and the distance from the fire to the spectators. Although the spectators might know about its benefits, the area is so spread out that they'll hardly smell the smoke.

The end result will be minimal unless a tremendous amount of currency is set on fire to produce much more smoke. The niche marketeer will have better results using the same amount of money because it's impact is targeted. Whether it's a baseball field, the printed media or the Internet the results will be the same. That is, it's much easier to attract the attention of a smaller crowd that you've identified as being interested in what you have to offer.

Plan your Marketing Strategy

So, why would you want to advertise your services to a niche market over a mass market? In other words, why would you want to target a smaller segment of your community over the entire community? Simple...It's more effective, less costly and produces better results. However, before you start burning up your cash for marketing efforts that might or might not work for you, it's imperative you plan your marketing strategy. The first thing that should be listed in your plan is the type and size niche you'll want to market.

Steps to Defining your Niche Market

First off, it's too expensive and usually a very difficult task to try and develop your own niche. It's better to identify and plan on addressing an existing niche that has good potential for using your unique product or services.

For example, let's assume you've invented a fantastic sports drink and want to develop the market for your product. Here are the first three steps you must take to find your niche:

— Assess yourself and determine what areas of life you are most interested in and how it will interface with your product.

— Assess your potential market to determine if there is an area that could use your services. An easy way to make this determination is just talk to the people in your targeted community. Another is to join groups of people who have similar interests such as health clubs, little league boosters, soccer clubs or at car racing activities.

Once you find a promising niche, then determine if you can be comfortable with the anticipated income from it. For example, if you decide to target sporting events, consider aligning yourself with local gyms or sports teams. Try to sponsor a series of community sporting events. Of course, an ample amount of samples should be available for your product's promotion.

BASIC CONCPETS FOR NICHE MARKETING SUCCESS

One common path to success for many small businesses is establishing themselves in a *niche market.* Because no matter how hard they try, no large retailer can provide all things to all people, there are always going to be segments of the population whose needs for particular products and/or services are going unmet – leaving room for the small business to succeed by meeting those needs.

So how can your small business capitalise on these unmet needs and find and dominate your own niche market? Concentrate on these four basic concepts for niche marketing success:

1. A Unique Product or Service

For starters, if you're going to master a niche market, you need to have a unique product or service. Ideally, you want to be the only one selling what you're selling.

The trick to coming up with such a product or service is to "look on the fringes" for unmet needs. For example, one East Coast entrepreneur's business consists of creating hand-made medieval outfits. Large retailers and even shops specialising in costumes don't supply these types of garments. Don't forget that processes can be products as well. They're ubiquitous now, but someone once looked at an inkjet printer cartridge and came up with the idea and the process for refilling them.

2. A Marketable Product or Service

You can create all kinds of wonderful and wonky products and/or services but if no one wants what you've produced, what's the point? Maybe there's no one selling fried insects from a vending cart on your street, but that doesn't mean it's a good idea. The niche market of people who enjoy eating fried insects in this country is so small they wouldn't even fill a phone booth.

There has to be enough of a demand for your product or service for your business to make a profit. How do you find out? By trial and error or by conducting extensive market research.

If you want to know if there's a market for dog coats, bamboo flooring or counselling for the Blackberry addicted, the best way to find out is to get out there and ask. Making or buying a lot of something and throwing up a Web site to see if there's any interest in what you're doing is for people who don't want to make money.

3. Choose a Niche Market that's Available

Remember, niche markets tend to be smaller so there's only room for so many players. When it comes to niche marketing, if you try to jump on a bandwagon, you're only going to fall off the back. Before you started such a business yourself, you would certainly need to carefully research the competition and the size of the market to see if a new business in this niche would be viable. It might well be better to find a different niche in the marriage or gay markets and make that niche your own.

4. Marketing

Marketing is perhaps more important for niche market businesses than for any other kind, because the niche market business is by definition, unknown and succeeds or fails on making the connection with exactly the right kind of customer/client. A unique product or service that will fulfil the unmet needs of a specific group of people – that's niche marketing in a nutshell. If you apply all of the four concepts above, your small business will enjoy the powerful competitive advantage that mastering a niche market provides.

HOW TO FIND AND SELL TO YOUR TARGET MARKET

Finding Your Target Market

The most successful small businesses understand that only a limited number of people will buy their product or service. The task then becomes determining, as closely as possible, exactly who those people are, and 'targeting' the business's marketing efforts and dollars toward them.

You, too, can build a better, stronger business, by identifying and serving a particular customer group – your target market. One of the first things you need to do is to refine your product or service so that you are not trying to be 'all things to all people.'

As a charter boat business, we knew that there were plenty of fishing charter operators in the area, and 'party boats' as well. So we decided that we would offer sightseeing or special event charters, and that we would not allow alcohol on board, or fishing rods. Yes, this decision eliminated a percentage of the market – but it also gave us a 'niche' that we could capitalise on, and expanded our market in a way that other charter operators could not take advantage of.

Next, you need to understand that people purchase products or services for three basic reasons:

— To satisfy basic needs.

— To solve problems.

— To make themselves feel good.

You'll need to determine which of those categories your product or service is the solution to, and be prepared to market it accordingly.

Your product or service may fit more than one category, too – our charter business primarily targets folks who just want to feel good – spending a day out on the water, relaxing and being waited on. But it also targets people who have visitors coming from out of town, or even overseas, because we represent a solution to the problem of "What will we do while our company is here? How can we entertain them, or show them our area?"

FIND YOUR OWN NICHE MARKET

Do you define the target market for your business similar to one of these? If you do, you're working harder and spending more money than necessary to promote your business. And you're enjoying only a fraction of the sales you should be getting.

Most business owners recognise the value of targeting a market. But when you target a broad audience like those listed above, you're only targeting prospects who can use your product or service. You have to narrow your focus if you want to target prospects who are likely to use your product or service. One of the best ways to do this is to find a niche market.

A niche market is a narrowly defined group that includes all of the following:

1. Individuals in the group have the same specialised interests and needs.
2. They have a strong desire for what you offer.
3. You have (or you can create) a compelling reason for prospects in the group to do business with you instead of with someone else.
4. You can easily reach individual prospects within the group.
5. The group is large enough to produce the volume of business you need.
6. The group is small enough that your competition is likely to overlook it.

Why You Must Narrow Your Focus

A niche market enables you to target your sales messages with great precision. The more narrowly you define your niche market the easier it is to cater to the specifically defined interests of people in that market. For example, some businesses describe their target market as "opportunity seekers". But this is a broad audience. You cannot cater to specifically defined personal interests of individuals in this group because it may include all of the following:

— Executives who want to get out of the corporate environment and start their own business

— New mothers who want to start a home based business

— Students who want to generate some extra income

Any promotional message to this group would have to be very general. But people don't respond to general talk. They respond only when they feel you are talking directly to them about their individual needs. A highly defined, small niche market can insulate you from competition. Other small businesses are likely to overlook it. Large businesses will find the market segment too small to bother with.

How To Find Your Own Niche Market

One way to find a good niche market is to evaluate your existing customers. Can you uncover a segment of customers with similar characteristics? Another way to find a niche market is to work backward from the benefits you offer. Start by listing all the benefits provided by your product or service. Then list some of the characteristics of prospects whose current situation can be dramatically improved by those benefits. You should begin to see a narrowly defined group emerge as a niche market.

10

HOW TO PROFITS FROM BUSINESS NETWORKING

Business networking is the process of establishing a mutually beneficial relationship with other business people and potential clients and/or customers. The key to true business networking is the establishment of a mutually beneficial relationship, and that's an incredibly rare event at the standard shake-hands-and-exchange-your-business-card events that are touted as business networking "opportunities".

The purpose of business networking is to increase business revenue—one way or another. The thickening of the bottom line can be immediately apparent, as in developing a relationship with a new client, or develop over time, as in learning a new business skill. The best business networking groups operate as exchanges of business information, ideas, and support.

The most important skill for effective business networking is listening; focusing on how you can help the person you are listening to rather than on how he or she can help you is the first step to establishing a mutally beneficial relationship.

NETWORKING ON THE NET

Networking is one of the most effective ways to find clients for any consulting or professional services business. But if you limit your networking to only what you can do in person, you'll be missing out on a huge number of possibilities.

Networking is more than entering a room full of people and exchanging business cards. It's creating a pool of contacts with whom you can exchange clients, referrals, resources, ideas, and information. Networking can happen by phone, by mail, over coffee, and increasingly, over the Internet.

The growth of the Internet has created many new ways to network without ever leaving your home or office. Pick a topic, any topic, and there will be multiple web sites and online communities devoted to it. Almost any type of Internet presence offers opportunities for networking.

In your favourite search engine, type the name of your profession or speciality, such as "interior design" or "marketing communications." Or, if you have a clearly defined target market, you can use that, such as "baby boomers" or "biotechnology." Skip the sponsored links or banner ads and focus on the detailed results.

What you will find is Internet networking opportunities such as the following:

Professional associations and schools—Many association or school sites provide member rosters, resource pages, back issues of newsletters, event calendars, and bulletin boards or discussion lists. Not all of these features will be restricted to members or students.

Resource sites and online communities—These include directories of people in the profession, vendors, articles, event calendars, bulletin boards, discussion lists, live chats, and links to even more resource sites.

Publications—Magazines and newsletters maintain sites that offer everything from back issues to complete online communities.

Job postings—These may appear on any of the above sites, and often include opportunities for independent professionals, not just those looking for full-time employment.

Colleagues and competitors—Colleagues and competitors may be exactly the same people, depending on your relationship with them. Their sites will tell you more about them and their work, and may offer many of the same features as resource sites.

Potential clients--Their sites will tell you about the work they do, current and upcoming projects, and even the names of executives and managers.

Now, how can you use all this information for Internet networking? Here are some of the most common ways:

Bulletin boards—These are web pages where you can view and post questions and comments on a specific subject. Answering a posted question is an excellent way to demonstrate your expertise, become known to the people who frequent the board, and get to know others in your field.

Don't be overly self-promotional when posting, just include a signature line at the end of your post, such as "Ingrid Gustafsson, Nordic Design." If you see someone else on the board who you would like to get to know in a collegial way, e-mail them. But never directly approach for business the people you find there. You might find yourself banned from membership.

COMMANDMENTS OF NETWORKING

Getting the Most Out of Business Networking

Business networking is when a group of like minded business people gather and help each other. If you check, you will surely find a networking group in your area. The networking group can meet as often as they wish, as is convenient for the participants.

Regretably, most people start with a networking group by looking for immediate gains.... that is, for favourable results for themselves. If this is what you are trying to achieve, you are networking for the wrong reasons and will be sticking out like a sore thumb.

Many people think that the size of a networking group makes the difference in networking. When groups start falling in size, members will say, "we have to build up our numbers." Now, what numbers are they referring to? Is it the number of participants? It is not the quantity, it is the quality.

Networking groups will come and go. To get the most out of your networking experience, you need to build a relationship with people who you want to have contact with. Not all members will be able to help you, nor will you be able to help them. When networking, spend most of your time and effort on people who can help each other out, for the long term. That is right. This is a long term project.

You will find that a highly effective networker will "work the net". The highly effective networker will take the time to cultivate a rapport. After the business networking event is when the real work begins. After all, you are only at the networking event to meet and build rapport. Follow up ASAP. Now is the time to send a nice customised card, and call a few days after to arrange a time to meet for a coffee or to have lunch. That is when you can listen to the details of what your new "friend" requires. You might even have the chance to offer your goods and services, only after listening.

If you want to gain the most out of business networking, follow the Ten Commandments of Networking!

1) Thou shalt drop the "what is in it for me?" attitude.
2) Thou shalt listen.
3) Thou shalt build a relationship.
4) Thou shalt give the first referral.
5) Thou shalt not tell others of the referral you require; thou shalt "show them" with a story.
6) Thou shalt be specific of the type of referral.
7) Thou shalt reciprocate when appropriate.
8) Thou shalt participate in the network executive, functions, and network time.
9) Thou shalt thank the person who gave a referral.
10) Thou shalt follow up on the referral within 24 hours.

Business networking is productive and fun, and that is why it will always be part of the Bigger Picture.

PROFIT FROM NETWORKING

Sales are frequently developed through the relationships we have created with other people. Networking functions provide the opportunity to expand our contact list, particularly when we create and nurture quality relationships. It is not enough to visit a networking group, talk to dozens of people and gather as many business cards possible. However, every networking function has tremendous potential for new business leads. Here are five strategies to make networking profitable:

1. *Choose the right networking group or event.* The best results come from attending the appropriate networking events for your particular industry. This should include trade shows, conferences, and associations dedicated to your type of business. For example, if your target market is a Fortune 500 company, it does not make sense to join a group whose primary membership consists of individual business owners.

   You can also participate in groups where your potential clients meet. A friend of mine helps people negotiate leases with their landlords. He joined the local franchise association because most franchisors lease their properties.

2. *Focus on quality contacts versus quantity.* Most people have experienced the person who, while talking to you, keeps his eyes roving around the room, seeking his next victim. This individual is more interested in passing out and collecting business cards than establishing a relationship.

3. *Make a positive first impression.* You have exactly one opportunity to make a great first impression. Factors that influence this initial impact are your handshake, facial expressions, eye contact, interest in the other person and your overall attentiveness. Develop a great handshake, approach people with a natural, genuine smile and make good eye contact. Notice the colour of the other person's eyes as you introduce yourself. Listen carefully to their name. If you don't hear them or understand exactly what they say, ask them to repeat it. Many people do not

speak clearly or loudly enough and others are very nervous at networking events. Make a powerful impression by asking them what they do before talking about yourself or your business. As Stephen Covey states, "Seek first to understand and then to be understood." Comment on their business, ask them to elaborate, or have them explain something in more detail. As they continue, make sure you listen intently to what they tell you. Once you have demonstrated interest in someone else, they will – in most cases – become more interested in you. When that occurs, follow the step outline in the next point.

4. *Be able to clearly state what you do.* Develop a ten second introduction as well as a thirty second presentation. The introduction explains what you do and for whom.

   Each of these introductions needs to be well-rehearsed so you can recite them at any time and under any circumstance.

5. *Follow up after the event.* The follow-up is the most important aspect of networking. There are two specific strategies to follow:

   — First, immediately after the event – typically the next day – you should send a handwritten card to the people you met. Mention something from your conversation and express your interest to keep in contact. Always include a business card in your correspondence.

   — Next, within two weeks, contact that person and arrange to meet for coffee or lunch. This will give you the opportunity to learn more about their business, the challenges they face, and how you could potentially help them. This is not a sales call – it is a relationship building meeting.

Networking does produce results. The more people know about you and your business, and the more they trust you, the greater the likelihood they will either work with you or refer someone else to you.

11

SECRETS OF GOOD CUSTOMER SERVICE

Excellent customer service is the ability of an organisation to constantly and consistently exceed the customer's expectations. Accepting this definition means expanding our thinking about customer service; if we're going to consistently exceed customers' expectations, we have to recognise that every aspect of our business has an impact on customer service, not just those aspects of our business that involve face-to-face customer contact.

Improving customer service involves making a commitment to learning what our customers' needs and wants are, and developing action plans that implement customer friendly processes.

TYPES OF CUSTOMERS

Increase your Loyal Customers to Increase your Sales

In the retail industry, it seems as though we are constantly faced with the issue of trying to find new customers. Most of us are obsessed with making sure our advertising, displays, and pricing all "scream out" to attract new customers. This focus on pursuing new customers is certainly prudent and necessary, but, at the same time, it can wind up hurting us. Therefore, our focus really should be on the 20 percent of our clients who currently are our best customers.

In retail, this idea of focusing on the best current customers should be seen as an on-going opportunity. To better understand the rationale behind this theory and to face the challenge of building customer loyalty, we need to break down shoppers into five main types:

— *Loyal customers:* They represent no more than 20 percent of our customer base, but make up more than 50 percent of our sales.

— *Discount customers:* They shop our stores frequently, but make their decisions based on the size of our markdowns.

— *Impulse customers:* They do not have buying a particular item at the top of their "To Do" list, but come into the store on a whim. They will purchase what seems good at the time.

— *Need-Based customers:* They have a specific intention to buy a particular type of item.

— *Wandering customers:* They have no specific need or desire in mind when they come into the store. Rather, they want a sense of experience and/or community.

If we are serious about growing our business, we need to focus our effort on the loyal customers, and merchandise our store to leverage the impulse shoppers. The other three types of customers do represent a segment of our business, but they can also cause us to misdirect our resources if we put too much emphasis on them.

Loyal Customers

Naturally, we need to be communicating with these customers on a regular basis by telephone, mail, email, etc. These people are the ones who can and should influence our buying and merchandising decisions. Nothing will make a Loyal Customer feel better than soliciting their input and showing them how much you value it. In my mind, you can never do enough for them. Many times, the more you do for them, the more they will recommend you to others.

Discount Customers

This category helps ensure your inventory is turning over and, as a result, it is a key contributor to cash flow. This same group, however, can often wind up costing you money because they are more inclined to return product.

Impulse Customers

Clearly, this is the segment of our clientele that we all like to serve. There is nothing more exciting than assisting an Impulse shopper and having them respond favorably to our recommendations. We want to target our displays towards this group because they will provide us with a significant amount of customer insight and knowledge.

Need-Based Customers

People in this category are driven by a specific need. When they enter the store, they will look to see if they can have that need filled quickly. If not, they will leave right away. They buy for a variety of reasons such as a specific occasion, a specific need, or an absolute price point. As difficult as it can be to satisfy these people, they can also become Loyal Customers if they are well taken care of. Salespeople may not find them to be a lot of fun to serve, but, in the end, they can often represent your greatest source of long-term growth.

It is important to remember that Need-Based Customers can easily be lost to Internet sales or a different retailer. To overcome this threat, positive personal interaction is required, usually from one of your top salespeople. If they are treated to a level of service not available from the Web or another retail location, there is a very strong chance of making them Loyal Customers. For this reason, Need-Based Customers offer the greatest long-term potential, surpassing even the Impulse segment.

Wandering Customers

For many stores, this is the largest segment in terms of traffic, while, at the same time, they make up the smallest percentage of sales. There is not a whole lot you can do about this group because the number of Wanderers you have is driven more by your store location than anything else.

Keep in mind, however, that although they may not represent a large percentage of your immediate sales, they are a real voice for you in the community. Many Wanderers shop merely for the interaction and experience it provides them. Shopping is no different to them than it is for another person to go to the gym on a regular basis. Since they are merely looking for interaction, they are also very likely to communicate to others the experience they had in the store. Therefore, although Wandering Customers cannot be ignored, the time spent with them needs to be minimised.

Retail is an art, backed up by science. The science is the information we have from financials to research data (the "backroom stuff"). The art is in how we operate on the floor: our merchandising, our people, and, ultimately, our customers. For all of us, the competitive pressure has never been greater and it is only going to become more difficult. To be successful, it will require patience and understanding in knowing our customers and the behavior patterns that drive their decision-making process.

Using this understanding to help turn Discount, Impulse, Need-Based, and even Wandering Customers into Loyal ones will help grow our business. At the same time, ensuring that our Loyal Customers have a positive experience each time they enter our store will only serve to increase our bottom-line profits.

RULES FOR GOOD CUSTOMER SERVICE

Good Customer Service Made Simple

Good customer service is the lifeblood of any business. You can offer promotions and slash prices to bring in as many new customers as you want, but unless you can get some of those customers to come back, your business won't be profitable for long.

Good customer service is all about bringing customers back. And about sending them away happy – happy enough to pass positive feedback about your business along to others, who may then try the product or service you offer for themselves and in their turn become repeat customers.

If you're a good salesperson, you can sell anything to anyone once. But it will be your approach to customer service that determines whether or not you'll ever be able to sell that person anything else. The essence of good customer service is forming a relationship with customers – a relationship that that individual customer feels that he would like to pursue.

How do you go about forming such a relationship? By remembering the one true secret of good customer service and acting accordingly; "You will be judged by what you do, not what you say."

1) Answer your phone

Get call forwarding. Or an answering service. Hire staff if you need to. But make sure that someone is picking up the phone when someone calls your business.

2) Don't make promises unless you WILL keep them

Not plan to keep them. Will keep them. Reliability is one of the keys to any good relationship, and good customer service is no exception. If you say, "Your new bedroom furniture will be delivered on Tuesday", make sure it is delivered on Tuesday. Otherwise, don't say it. The same rule applies to client appointments, deadlines, etc.. Think before you give any promise – because nothing annoys customers more than a broken one.

3) Listen to your customers

Is there anything more exasperating than telling someone what you want or what your problem is and then discovering that that person hasn't been paying attention and needs to have it explained again? Can the sales pitches and the product babble. Let your customer talk and show him that you are listening by making the appropriate responses, such as suggesting how to solve the problem.

4) Deal with complaints

No one likes hearing complaints, and many of us have developed a reflex shrug, saying, "You can't please all the people all the time". Maybe not, but if you give the complaint your attention, you may be able to please this one person this one time - and position your business to reap the benefits of good customer service.

5) Be helpful - even if there's no immediate profit in it.

6) Train your staff (if you have any) to be ALWAYS helpful, courteous, and knowledgeable

Do it yourself or hire someone to train them. Talk to them about good customer service and what it is (and isn't) regularly. Most importantly, give every member of your staff enough information and power to make those small customer-pleasing decisions, so he never has to say, "I don't know, but so-and-so will be back at..."

7) Take the extra step

For instance, if someone walks into your store and asks you to help them find something, don't just say, "It's in Aisle 3." Lead the customer to the item. Better yet, wait and see if he has questions about it, or further needs. Whatever the extra step may be, if you want to provide good customer service, take it. They may not say so to you, but people notice when people make an extra effort and will tell other people.

8) Throw in something extra

Whether it's a coupon for a future discount, additional information on how to use the product, or a genuine smile, people love to get more than they thought they were getting. And don't think that a gesture has to be large to be effective. The local art framer that we use attaches a package of picture hangers to every picture he frames. A small thing, but so appreciated.

If you apply these eight simple rules consistently, your business will become known for its good customer service. And the best part? The irony of good customer service is that over time it will bring in more new customers than promotions and price slashing ever did!

WAYS TO PROVIDE SUCCESSFUL CUSTOMER SERVICE

Bring them Back with Shiny Customer Service

There's no real secret to getting your customers to come back. All you need to do is provide customer service that exceeds your customers' expectations and outshines your competitors' customer service. In Canada, Acumen Research Group surveyed more than 1,000 retail, banking and telco customers to determine what made them behave loyally and what made them leave long-term relationships; 43 percent of respondents abandoned a provider to which they declared themselves loyal because of a negative experience with a staff person, and 30 percent of respondents reported that having the feeling they are not treated as valued customers by the staff has been the main reason for taking their business elsewhere.

Shiny customer Service is service with a capital "S", Service that makes your customer feel special, Service that makes him or her want to come back and do more business with your company, and recommend your business to his or her friends. So how can you provide customer Service that shines? Follow this plan to ensure customer service that will dazzle customers and competitors alike:

1) Determine what makes what you offer special

Think about their customer service and the customer service you provide. What can you offer your customers that is "better" than the competition? There are sure to be aspects of your customer Service that you can promote as "Special".

Make a list of all these ideas for providing customer service. If you sell a product, and your competitor doesn't offer it already, perhaps you can offer free local delivery. If you sell a service, such as bookkeeping or accounting, perhaps you can focus on turnaround times that are faster than your competitors'—providing the good customer service that will give your business the edge.

Sometimes providing customer Service that shines will involve expanding your operations. For instance, you may need to offer to provide your services in customer's homes to outdo the services the competition provides.

Sometimes providing customer Service that shines will involve revamping what you've always done. If you provide a service that involves giving estimates of the job to be done beforehand, and you've previously just given estimates to prospective customers orally, you could stress that you provide an estimate in writing and stick to your written estimate. Remember, we're talking about customer Service here. Lower prices are not service; they're just lower prices.

Continue on to the next page to read more ideas for providing customer service that will help you outshine the customer service your competitors provide.

Putting Your Customer Service Ideas Into Action

Now that you have a list of customer service ideas that you might use to provide customer service that outshines the customer service your competitors provide, it's time to look at implementing shiny customer service.

2) Study the customer service ideas on your list and examine their feasibility

Can you really guarantee that you will always stick to your written estimate or provide a faster turnaround time than your competitors? If you aren't sure, or can't do it, cross it off your customer service ideas list. Customer service that shines carries that same kind of guarantee; it's not a "sometimes" proposition. So only choose what you can definitely do one hundred percent of the time.

3) Choose one or two of your shiny customer service ideas and implement them

Feature this aspect of your customer service in whatever ads you run, including your yellow pages listing. Put it on your business cards and in your email signature. Make it part of your greeting spiel when you answer the phone.

You need to make your customer service a prominent feature of every ad too, so people automatically associate it with your business.

While one of the big payoffs of your shiny customer service will be the great word-of-mouth advertising it generates, this takes time, and you need to help it along by getting the word out. Don't be shy! Solicit customer service testimonials from satisfied customers, that you can use in print ads, such as in newspapers, ezines, and on your website, if you have one, or can at least use as references for new potential customers.

4) Stay proactive and keep gathering customer service ideas

Listen to your customers and find out what kind of special customer service they want. You can do this formally, by creating a customer satisfaction feedback form that you enclose with every sale or post on your website, or informally, by asking them for their customer service ideas when they're in your store or office. Shiny customer service is service that's responsive to customers' needs.

Customers are tired of dealing with retailers that ignore customer service or only pretend to have it, and as always, they're voting with their dollars. Shiny customer Service will draw customers to your product or service, rather than a competitors', and bring them back in droves.

Client Relationship Management

Tension arises with clients when expectations are not met in the eyes of the client. If this is not possible, it is not worth doing business with the client, whether you are doing sales, marketing or development work. Below are a number of client relationship management lessons.

Lesson 1: Call the client

When things go wrong and the client knows, call. Email does not always translate circumstances or feelings well as there is no voice inflection and a client usually places more value on a phone call. Discuss the situation and have solutions ready! Also have a time line ready for implementing the solutions and resolving the problems. Be sure you can deliver on the timeline; this will restore confidence. People in crises situations feel less stress when they know what to expect. When you execute the solutions and the client is aware of this they will increase their confidence in you and relax more.

Lesson 2: Keep the client informed

When things go wrong and the client doesn't know, it is still a good idea to let them know. This is not always the case, but in my experience, more often than not it resolves more potential problems than it causes and shows your integrity.

Lesson 3: Offer solutions

Have solutions ready for clients when there are problems. Do not expect them to tell you what to do. Offer them solutions and ask for their thoughts. In my case clients have most often said, "What do you think we should do?" This shows the client that you have thought about the problem and have it under control.

Lesson 4: Watch those promises

Do not promise what you cannot deliver. It is always better to "under promise and over deliver" as they say. This is critical in the above scenarios and always true with clients. Set realistic timelines and budgets and add a little padding so you can absolutely deliver what you promised and then some. This will pay off in spades. Clients will be more likely to refer you and more likely to use you in the future.

Lesson 5: Add value

Add value to you and your business by bringing the client ideas. New pitches, marketing strategies, anything that is of value that will help move the client's business forward will be appreciated. This may lead to additional dollars in your contract and increased loyalty. The drawback comes when a client starts spending a lot of your time talking about new ideas. It is important to be careful with this one. Be sure that the relationship is set up so everyone respects one another's time. When applied with tact these client relationship management lessons will help you minimise conflict as it arises and add value to you in your clients' eyes.

12

STRATEGIC MARKET MANAGEMENT

Marketing management requires sufficient powers and authority to effectively manage the market. These should include powers to determine the following:

- rental fees and charges;
- minimum quantities;
- hours of operation;
- access to the market;
- traffic and parking controls;
- produce unloading, loading and stacking;
- produce movement;
- allocation procedures;
- ability to enter into contracts and agreements (e.g. for rental of space and for market cleaning).

MARKET RULES, CONTRACTS AND AGREEMENTS

Market rules and regulations should be impartially, fairly, but effectively enforced. Failure to do so can lead to congestion or confusion in the market as well as to poor hygiene and costly operations for most market users.

Economic Viability and Sustainability

The managing authority must develop a business plan, an annual work plan and an annual budget. The budget, based on the business and work plans, should ensure that income generated is sufficient to meet all operational costs, as well as to provide funds (in reserve) for long-term maintenance, capital replacement and reserves for staff benefits.

Effective Relationships with Market Users, Service Providers, Government Agencies and other Markets

Conflicts can arise unless there is a strong commitment by traders to the market and an understanding of what the managing authority is seeking to achieve (e.g. if changes or increased fees are proposed). Similarly, if a government agency has to approve the budget, loans or penalties there must be an understanding of why the proposals are made and the need for a timely decision. Also, as mentioned, a market is dependent for success on the efficient operations of other markets and market centres such as collection facilities and packing houses. Effective consultation, representation and coordination arrangements thus need to be put in place by the managing authority with market users, service providers, transport operators, government agencies and other markets.

Operational and Managerial Efficiency

The management and staff of the managing authority must be committed to the operation of an efficient market. This will require that the market opens on time, that traffic and parking is controlled, that produce handling and movement is efficient, that space is used appropriately without interfering with the rights of others, that market cleaning and garbage disposal is carried out regularly (at least on a daily basis) and that facilities are maintained (e.g. toilets, drinking water, telephones, fax, e-mail and support facilities such as cold stores).

Effective Decision-making Structure

The board of directors of the managing authority must be capable of making decisions, which can be implemented. This requires an understanding of the objectives, programmes and plans of the organisation. It requires effective understanding of the role of the market and the need for consultation and communication with market tenants, users and service providers, government agencies and other market managers.

It requires having an efficient management and staff team. It requires each staff member to know his or her duties and how these are to be carried out. Staff need to know what should be referred to the board of directors for policy or decision. Also, it means that the board of directors must have the necessary facts for effective decision making. This will require a meeting agenda which provides for optimal decisions which can be taken in minimum time. The board of directors has a responsibility to ensure that management fully implement the programmes, plans and decisions of the board in a timely and cost effective manner.

Trained and Disciplined Staff

Market staff need to be well-trained in order to know what they are to do to meet the managing authority's objectives and plans and to implement the board's decisions. Staff require supervision to ensure their approach is disciplined and structured. Financial accountability, conscientious attendance and impartiality, fairness and consistent firmness in ensuring that market rules are observed are all essential to efficient market operations.

Integrity of Wholesalers

Growers who wish to supply produce to a market need to have confidence in the market and its integrity - especially as regards their transactions with wholesalers. Usually the managing authority is not directly responsible for ensuring compliance with government commercial law. However, it will be necessary to take some initiative if a wholesaler is reported as consistently failing to pay suppliers the right amounts of money or to pay on time. Any evidence that a particular wholesaler may be running into financial difficulties or even bankruptcy can affect the market and hence potential market revenue, including managing authority income.

Politics and Finance

Markets subject to political intervention in terms of staff placements, allocation of space to traders or to financial 'kickbacks' inevitably become poorly managed and poorly supported by suppliers and buyers. Also, overly ambitious capital development programmes requiring large funding from reserves or loans can result in an overcapitalised market not able to be sustained by income from rentals. Market expansion, which requires large capital investment, should be based on predetermined demand and a precommitment agreement with the expected users of the new facilities.

MARKET MANAGEMENT

Principles

A wholesale market will be judged on the following criteria:

1. Financial viability of the market reflecting confidence and trust in its use, and acceptance of its fees and charges and rules by wholesalers, retail and other buyers and users.
2. Operational efficiency, including:
   — efficient handling of the arrival, unloading and loading of produce;
   — discipline in the market in the internal movement, storage and display of produce, which is achieved through enforceable tenancy agreements, and widely accepted and implemented market regulations or rules;
   — traffic control and vehicle parking;
   — personal safety;
   — produce security;
   — cleanliness and hygiene;
   — effective provision of services, such as loading and unloading services, produce movement, electricity, garbage collection, telephone, fax, e-mail, and internal communications, warehousing and cold storage.
3. A pleasant and safe trading and working environment in which private trading can operate profitably.
4. The extent to which the market meets general community needs by ensuring:
   — a regular supply of products in the necessary quantities and quality;

— transparency in price setting through free competition between traders;

— that standards and grades are adhered to, where relevant;

— that packaging meets the needs of the market and of the eventual consumers.

5. The relationship of the management authority with market users, including wholesalers, other market operators, and suppliers, retailers, and other buyers and service providers.

Contractual Agreements with Market Users

Most management authorities have contractual agreements with persons renting space in the market in order to clearly define rights and obligations. This is to ensure discipline in market operations, and to minimise misunderstandings leading to costly legal disputes and litigation. For occasional or casual users this can take the form of terms and conditions printed on a ticket or permit which is issued on payment of a fee. Often a statement acknowledging acceptance of, and willingness to comply with, the terms and conditions of market rules is included for signature by the users. Failure to comply can lead to the managing authority refusing to allow access to selling space or to allow access only on restricted conditions.

For longer term wholesalers and other market tenants the managing authority usually enters into a specific contract with each tenant. This is frequently a lease or rental agreement which gives the managing authority absolute final control over the premises. In general, such an agreement should specify:

— the area to be rented or leased (ground lease: space in building described by area, position, number, etc);

— the rental or fees to be paid, when they are to be paid (e.g. monthly, by the first of the month, in advance), where they are to be paid;

— penalties or charges for failure to pay by due date;

— the period or duration of the rental or lease;

— arrangements or options for renewal of the agreement (when provisions of existing agreement have been observed);

— procedures for adjustment to fees to cover inflation or other cost increases. Most usually this is done with reference to an independent index (e.g. cost of living index) or to an agreed percentage at regular intervals. Occasionally, arbitration may be provided for;

— that the lease or rental should apply only to the particular person, firm or partnership, or company while engaged in the approved business (e.g. wholesaling of fruit and vegetables) and only as long as the particular person/firm remains licensed for this purpose (with the relevant authority);

— arrangements for subletting. Usually subletting is prohibited and is only allowed by prior approval in writing from the managing authority (otherwise the agreement is considered void);

— proscription of modifications (including signs) to the premises without prior written approval of the managing authority. Any modification becomes the property of the managing authority;

— repairs to premises. They may be at the cost of the tenant or the authority, and this responsibility needs to be clearly understood and stated;

— arrangements for supply of electricity, water, sewerage, telephone, fax, e-mail, security, cleaning and maintenance, and payment arrangements;

- action in event of non-payment of fees or failure to comply with the market rules. This constitutes a breach of contract and the contract is usually automatically terminated with the building returning to the control of the managing authority;
- penalties for breaches of market rules. Failure to pay these will result in termination of the contract (some markets insist on traders paying a security deposit from which fines are deducted);
- compliance with licensing requirements;
- market inspection. The authority should have an agreed access to the lessee's premises;
- staff employed. It is usually required that they remain on the rented space;
- guarantees (i.e. who will supply any financial guarantees);
- legal costs. The agreement should specify who will pay these in the event of dispute.

Enforcement of Market Rules

Rules and regulations

Markets are places for the interaction of various interest groups and individuals seeking to optimise their revenue. Markets therefore need to be managed with an impartiality, which recognises the importance of all users for its successful operation. However, in a competitive environment there will be inevitably conflicts, and chaos and confusion which can be to the detriment of the weaker participants unless there are clear and concise market rules or regulations and strict and consistent enforcement of them.

These rules or regulations should be clear, practical and as simple as possible so that they are easily understood and implemented. The reasons for the particular regulation should be understood by all users of the market. They should be drafted by the managing authority in close consultation with market user groups to ensure their practicality. They must take account of national and municipal laws and be within the power and authority given in law and in any enabling legislation, order, or legal instrument establishing the managing authority.

Further, the penalties or sanctions to enforce regulations or rules must also be within the power and authority of the managing authority, or be provided for in legislation or regulation. For example, if it is proposed to have "on-the-spot" fines for parking offences this power may need to be given or delegated by the provincial or municipal government by inclusion in their legislation or regulations.

Ensure compliance

The most practical way to ensure compliance with market rules is to have the market users, through their representatives, involved in the drafting process. Peer or group pressure within the market can mean that for most of the time rules are observed. For example, if a wholesaler consistently stacks produce on the market floor or pavement area outside of the space leased by him then other wholesalers who are disadvantaged or hindered in their business will seek to correct the situation. There must be clearly understood procedures for action to be taken by the managing authority. Staff must be clearly designated as responsible for specific activities such as enforcement of rules applying to loading and unloading and the stacking of produce in walkways, loading areas and other common-use areas.

These staff must have the delegated power and authority to act. Action normally consists of a first warning to remove the offending produce. If that order is not complied with the offender should be penalised, either by the removal of the produce to a holding area by market staff (with recovery on payment of costs and a fine) or by issue of a breach notice, leading to the penalty authorised in the rules. In some persistent cases the matter may be taken by the chief executive officer to the board of the managing authority and the board may impose a larger fine, if provided for in the rules.

In extreme cases the board may require the tenant to show cause why the lease agreement should not be terminated as a result of failure to comply with the provisions of the contract. However, before this action is contemplated the board should call the offender into a meeting. In some situations the tenant may face a practical problem which needs to be addressed by the managing authority. For example, bad layout may give poor access to floor space in a particular location.

Legal issues

What is included in the market rules will depend on a number of factors:

— the legal competency or powers and authority delegated by government to the managing authority;

— whether there is a legal lease or rental agreement or contract between the managing authority and market tenants and the coverage of that agreement. It is not desirable for the rules to duplicate provisions of contracts;

— the functions undertaken by the managing authority. For example, if the authority reserves the sole right to undertake all loading and unloading services in the market then the market rules must specify this;

— if there are several commodity groups in a supply centre, then separate rules will usually be necessary for each delivery and trading arrangements are usually different;

— if the rules are difficult to be amended (e.g. requiring government or parliamentary approval), then the rules themselves may provide that actual practical regulations be made by decision of the board (e.g. the market rules may state that market entry "shall be as determined by the board from time to time"). A decision of the board given as a notice to the all tenants in the market would specify the actual hours when vehicles and persons may enter the market.

Issues in drafting

A number of issues must be considered in the development and drafting of market rules and regulations. This section identifies the major issues and offers specific comments that will be of help in this undertaking. These are:

— market trading days;

— market hours and market access;

— authorised produce trading;

— minimum quantities;

— allocation of space;

— ancillary functions;

— vehicle movement and parking;

— produce handling;

— quality and packaging;

— wholesaler activities;

— cleaning and garbage disposal;

— licensing;

— fees and charges;

— penalities;

— other matters

Market trading days. A major decision to be made is on which days, if any, the market is to be closed. This should be done in consultation with government as well as with the users.

Market hours and market access. Market rules generally need to cover three specific areas in relation to market hours:

— hours for delivery and collection of produce;

— hours for entry of people including wholesale, their staff, licensed buyers (if appropriate) and the general public;

— hours of trading

Some markets seek to restrict trading hours which, in effect, is a restriction only on produce movement. Much trading activity in markets now takes place by telephone, fax or e-mail. This is difficult and not particularly desirable to regulate. The reasons for wanting to restrict trading hours need to be clearly understood by the managing authority and accepted by the market overall. These could include security, market cleaning requirements and life-style choices of wholesalers (not wanting to operate all day). However, decisions to restrict trading hours will mean that the board also has to make decisions on the following:

— a time after which movement of produce to selling floor areas is not permitted;

— times at which produce may enter or be moved from or to warehouse storage areas located elsewhere in the market, including delivery to facilities controlled by supermarkets within or outside the market.

Decisions on these matters will have an impact on decisions with regard to entry of vehicles loaded with produce and entry of people into the market as well as in respect of produce collection and exit. Hours of entry of vehicles with produce will depend on:

— areas and distances from which vehicles have to travel;

— whether any general or specific conditions apply such as checkpoints or government regulations on heavy vehicle movement inside cities. It is self-evident that times of entry of vehicles into a market must be consistent with permitted times of access to the city;

— whether loads are palletised, unitised (i.e. one product for one wholesaler) or consist of mixed loads of produce for various selling floors. Different trading hours may have to be applied to allow produce to be unloaded, sorted and delivered to sections before opening of trading;

— whether market design and layout requires trucks delivering produce to exit the market before the opening of trading and the arrival of buyer's vehicles;

Most markets require wholesalers and staff to park vehicles in designated areas away from trading floors. Some markets give, for a small annual fee, a special entrance privilege to registered buyers (i.e. retailers or larger institutional customers). This allows larger buyers to have access to loading areas and to inspect produce prior to general public access.

Whether separate rules need to be developed in respect to the exit of vehicles with produce will depend on the hours of operation, the need for security of produce, and the need for a time when traffic is minimal to allow for market cleaning and/or orderly unloading.

In most markets information is obtained regarding quantities being delivered from vehicles entering with produce. Usually a copy of the driver's manifest (loading docket) is obtained and the date and time of arrival recorded. Where such manifests are unavailable and quality information is required, it may be necessary to follow other procedures. These, however, can often be time-consuming and delay access.

In some markets where access by buyers is not differentiated, registered buyers displaying appropriate stickers are allowed to back into loading ramps while cars of the general public are directed to other areas for parking.

Some markets allow wholesalers and their staff unrestricted access during daylight or specified hours, but require that prior approval be obtained for regular entry outside these hours. Emergency entry (e.g. to check produce arriving late or to service a cold store owned by the wholesaler) should be recorded by gate staff. Restrictions on entry are usually applied for security of produce or to enforce trading hour regulations.

Separate rules for hours of entry or operation may be developed for ancillary services such as cafés, restaurants, cold stores, prepacking plants, sorting or "picking-over" areas, warehouses, ripening rooms and other service areas.

Authorised produce trading. The market rules (as well as the tenancy agreement) should specify what produce may be sold in the space rented or leased. They may also prescribe the packaging required. For example, many Indian markets specify that fruit must be packaged in wooden boxes and must be sold in the boxes in which it arrives in the market.

Problems arise in markets where authorised produce is not specified. This often leads to wholesalers selling other produce, such as eggs or spices, in a fruit and vegetable market. In addition, the rules should specify that only authorised sellers of authorised products can trade in the market. This can be used to prevent itinerant sellers, including outside vendors, from operating in the market

Minimum quantities. The determination, within market rules, of what constitutes "wholesale" sales is difficult. Some markets specify that produce must be traded in the container in which it arrives (i.e. case, box, carton or bag). This approach usually requires that the acceptable containers be specified or approved by the managing authority.

Difficulties faced include how to deal with bulk deliveries or loose items. Large disposable bulk bins of fruit are now delivered to many wholesale markets. Usually these are sold on pallets and delivered to large retail stores. Sometimes, however, they are repacked into smaller packs. Loose larger items such as melons, pumpkins, cabbages and cauliflowers do not readily lend themselves to a concise definition of "wholesale" quantities.

Some markets make a simple distinction between wholesale and retail sales by establishing a minimum trading quantity for all produce. This leads to many anomalies. For example, 5 kilograms of garlic is a reasonably significant quantity, while 5 kilograms of watermelon can be one melon. However, such a blanket approach is sometimes preferred to the alternative of specifying and enforcing different minimum quantities for all items.

Some markets allow access to the general public after registered retail buyers have had prior access. At this time wholesale sales in smaller quantities may be permitted. However, as a general rule the preferred approach is to determine the package size and require sales in the container in which the produce arrives, with minimum quantities being specified for loose or bulk items.

Most markets have a rule or regulation, which empowers the managing authority to refuse a transfer in the following circumstances:

- to a person or company previously excluded from the market or other markets;
- to a person or company which has a history of insolvency or bankruptcy;
- to a person or company already owning or leasing a section or space (or nominated number of spaces) in the market.

Some markets specifically exclude persons engaged in retailing (including supermarkets) from owning or controlling wholesale space in the market. Where the managing authority seeks to restrict the allocation or transfer of a section or space on the grounds of a person having control of another space, it is important that there be a provision in the market rules clearly limiting the number of sections in which any one person may have an interest.

Provision should exist in the market rules for the transfer or cancellation of leases or licenses in the event of death, bankruptcy or liquidation of a company. Many markets have found it expedient to have a provision for cancellation of leases in these circumstances. Without the possibility of reissuing a lapsed lease, matters can take years to resolve and revenue is not earned for the space.

It is usual to include in the market rules a provision for cancellation of leases/licenses in cases of default on payments, unauthorised subletting or transfer of leases/ licenses; and for consistent offences in relation to operational management; or for serious misconduct (such as assaulting an employee of the market).

Once market operations are under way, the assignment of new or vacant market stalls to established or to new external wholesalers requires prior decisions on:

— whether to establish a maximum holding by one person/firm;

— whether introducing new wholesalers is desirable;

— the method of allocation (tender or lottery - tenders can be more acceptable in these circumstances than at the time of initial allocation).

In relation to the allocation of other facilities in the market (e.g. warehouses, cold rooms, ripening rooms and packaging or sorting rooms) separate contracts or lease agreements are usually entered into with persons using these facilities. These arrangements can be for a ground or land lease, with responsibility for construction by the successful tenderer or nominated company of a clearly defined building which may, in time, become the property of the managing authority. Such arrangements allow for management of these facilities independently of the selling floor areas. Also, separate contracts permit necessary additional or special conditions to be applied (e.g. responsibility for maintenance, management, access and security). Allocation of non-trading-floor space should normally be done by tender in order to maximise the market's revenue.

Sometimes management authorities build these facilities "on demand", for example, warehouse facilities may be constructed as a result of prior agreement with individual wholesalers to rent a specified area for a rental which would repay the investment over a period of, say, 10 to 15 years.

Ancillary facilities. The rules for ancillary facilities such as cold storage, warehouses and prepackaging areas will depend on the policy adopted in relation to their construction (i.e. who paid for these buildings). Those facilities located within the market complex, but independent of trading areas, should have separate market rules. General rules for cleaning can apply but these facilities should have their own operational rules or regulations, especially as regards opening hours for access to and for the movement of goods. In order to maintain management unity and security in the complex, it is preferable that access to these facilities be through the main entrances of the market, both for people and vehicles. The rules for these facilities should clearly determine whether they may be used by other than the lessee (e.g. for storage of produce owned by other traders). Either the market rules or the contract agreement should establish this right and provide for indemnities to the managing authority in the event of default, theft or loss. Operators of these facilities should be required to supply the same information on volumes handled and other matters as is required from market wholesalers.

Vehicle movement and parking. Markets should have a traffic control plan aimed at ensuring public safety, efficiency of produce handling, and optimal use of pavement and parking areas. This plan can be translated into operational plans for staff. The plan will also require some powers to be established within the market rules to allow staff to implement and enforce it. Issues to be addressed should include:

— hours and procedures for entry of vehicles with loads;

— designated unloading areas;

— duration vehicles may park in loading dock/ramp areas and the time by which they should leave these areas;

— exit of vehicles which have brought produce to the market;

— parking for buyers' vehicles, including time allowed at loading ramps/docks. (Note: one of the reasons some markets register retail buyers is to give parking permits which enable enforcement of parking rules by withdrawal of permits for consistent infringement.);

— entry and parking of wholesalers' and staff vehicles;

— entry and parking for cars and vehicles of the general public;

— parking fees;

— penalties for illegal parking or for use of an area larger than permitted, including "on-the-spot" fines. As mentioned, the legal environment may require municipal, provincial or national legislation to enable the market to impose penalties. A government may require a consistent approach in all public or quasi-public areas;

— hours of exit of vehicles, if market is to be closed;

— inspection of vehicles leaving to ensure appropriate documentation and to prevent theft of produce;

— registration of vehicles and equipment, such as forklifts, used by licensed drivers for produce movement in the market and creation of special roadways/alleyways for forklift movement.

Produce handling. This includes the unloading, on-section movement, movement between wholesalers, loading, stocking and display, and sorting of produce. Each of these is briefly described below.

Many market authorities have reserved for themselves, or for an organisation they appoint, the right for the *unloading* of produce. The reasons for this are to minimise confusion, to more economically utilise mechanical handling equipment, to reduce theft (for night arrivals), and to keep wholesaler presence in the market during night hours to a minimum. Market rules therefore can stipulate that unloading of vehicles should be done by the managing authority or by companies appointed or authorised by the authority.

"On-section" movement of produce within a rented space is the responsibility of the lessee/licensee. Market rules usually specify that a wholesaler must not stand produce outside the leased area.

In a busy market it is possible for many vehicles and forklifts to be used for produce *movement between wholesalers* and to and from warehouses and other facilities. Some markets, in their market rules, apply restrictions and conditions on the use of forklifts and vehicles operating in the market, requiring licensing or registration of such vehicles with the authority, licensing of drivers with the appropriate authorities, and training within the context of the market's traffic control plan.

Loading is usually done by retail buyers using their own vehicles with assistance from wholesaler's staff or the available loading service staff. Market rules often specify that larger vehicles (specified by size) must be loaded by the authorised service provider. This is to minimise loading time and optimise use of the loading ramps/docks.

Market rules regarding produce *stocking and display* usually specify that between certain hours (usually the formal trading hours) no wholesaler may stack or store produce outside his allocated selling floor space or warehouse space. A common provision is that produce which has been sold and is being delivered to trucks or other vehicles must be moved directly from the allocated space or warehouse to the vehicle and must not be stored or left outside the section, in passageways, on loading ramps or on the market pavement area.

As mentioned, penalties can include on-the-spot fines or seisure of the produce and its movement to a secure lock-up holding area with required payment of charges for its release. Market rules can provide that offenders who persistently interfere with the rights of other market users may be asked to show cause why their lease or license should not be cancelled. Market rules also usually require that a wholesaler should not store or display produce loosely in contact with the pavement or the ground for reasons of hygiene.

In nearly all markets some produce arrives which requires *sorting* or "picking-over". Because of the garbage problems this can create, many markets now require that this be done in a designated area. A fee for use of tables and equipment is charged. In some markets there is a service provider who will undertake the task of sorting produce and rebagging or placing it in new cartons or boxes.

Quality and packaging. Wholesale markets play an essential role in developing and maintaining quality standards for an industry. Often national quality standards and required packaging can be incorporated in national or provincial legislation and regulations. If so, then the responsibility for enforcement may rest with inspectors appointed under these regulations. In these circumstances the market authority's responsibility is to require that all produce supplied, sold and delivered in the market complies with legal standards. As well, access to wholesalers' premises must be ensured for authorised inspectors, by specifying this in market rules or in tenancy agreements.

If a market is used to assemble produce for supply to export markets then high-grade standards and strict quality control will be required. Government inspection and phytosanitary certification will be necessary and provision will need to be made for such certification procedures.

Wholesaler activities. The regulatory control of wholesaler activity usually rests with national, provincial or municipal governments. This is usually done through legislation or regulation which sets out the responsibilities of wholesalers, whether acting as merchants, brokers or commission agents. Often this is within the context of general commercial law.

A usual minimum requirement of wholesalers acting as merchants (i.e. buying fruit from a grower and selling it at a profit to a retailer) is as follows:

- — a receipt must be issued to the supplier indicating date, type of produce, description, (including grade standard), quantity, price agreed to or paid and any deductions agreed by the two parties (e.g. when the wholesaler has been asked to pay for freight costs);
- — a docket or invoice must be supplied to the buyer showing the date, produce supplied, quantity, price paid and other costs as agreed (e.g. delivery costs);

— the merchant must keep a carbon copy or computer record of all transactions.

Commission agents act as agents for the grower/supplier and physically handle the produce. Unlike merchants, the agents never legally own the produce. A fee or commission, usually a percentage of the sale price, is charged. Documentation usually required is a statement to the grower showing the date, produce supplied (including grade standard), the quantity, the price the goods were sold for, the commission and any other agreed charges deducted. A document is usually required to be supplied to the buyer as for a merchant transaction, but it should also record the supplier (this is often coded).

Brokers act as commission agents but do not usually physically handle the goods, arranging supply, sale and delivery by telephone, fax or e-mail. The fees charged are of the order of 2 or 3 percent compared to commission agent's rates, which range from 5 to 10 percent.

Market authorities usually require, through market rules, that licensed wholesalers supply daily information to them or some authorised agency on quantities traded and highest, lowest and most frequent prices for various commodities. Some markets also include a system where produce is offered for sale at auction. Those markets, which receive large quantities of perfectly graded produce and whose function is to redistribute goods to other sales outlets, carry out transactions by means of auction bidding using an electronic notice board.

Many markets, especially those with auction systems require some form of buyer registration in their market rules. This applies particularly where payments to the auction agent are to be on credit. Credit-guarantee schemes, which may be incorporated in market rules, can require registration of buyers, lodging of a fidelity bond, or bank or other financial-institution guarantee, and a follow-up system of suspension in the event of default on payments.

Market rules can provide for dispute resolution procedures on quantities, grades, and prices. Disputes can arise between a supplier and a wholesaler, between one wholesaler and another, between a retailer and a wholesaler, or with service providers such as transport operators. Market inspectors appointed by government may be used to resolve these disputes. In a few cases market staff may be used. However, increasingly these disputes are resolved either by independent arbitrators or by industry associations. Often the traders' association has developed a *code of practice* with which all members must comply. This code will include dispute-resolution arrangements. In these circumstances, market rules (and tenancy agreements) may state that all traders must be members of the traders' association and comply with its code of practice.

Cleaning and garbage disposal. Market rules require that tenants in the market are responsible for hygiene and cleaning of the spaces they occupy, and that they deposit refuse in places or containers specified. Some markets require tenants to be responsible for cleaning of a specified area outside the rented space. Sweeping or cleaning of most common areas, collecting garbage from containers or collection points and garbage disposal are responsibilities of the managing authority.

A common problem with use of a central waste collection point (e.g. ramp, dump area, or compactor) is that outside persons bring waste products and empty containers into the market. Market rules can stipulate that only wholesalers or registered tenants or their employees may place refuse or garbage in the central collection point.

Licensing. Apart from licences which some markets issue in relation to rented or leased trading areas, wholesalers may also be required to hold other licences or permits. These could include any licence required for a wholesaler to operate as a merchant, commission agent, broker, or auctioneer, or to own or use specific equipment (ripening rooms, forklift). Market rules and tenancy agreements should specify that all traders should obtain and hold the necessary licences. Failure to do so would result in suspension or cancellation of the tenancy or right to trade.

Fees and charges. Market rules and regulations usually set out in detail the following:

- — rental or lease fees for various facilities;
- — capital fee payments;
- — entry fees for buyers/suppliers (if any);
- — vehicle entry fees (if any);
- — commission rates for agency transactions;
- — auction fees;
- — special cleaning, packaging, produce grading fees (if not covered by rental or lease fees).

Penalties. Market rules and regulations should set out clearly the penalties and sanctions which apply in the event of failure to comply with a particular requirement. These can include financial penalties, "on-the-spot" fines, authority to cancel or suspend leases or licenses or, in the event of specific or consistent offences, to reduce the area to be leased.

Other matters. There are a number of other matters which may be included in market rules, such as:

- — arbitration or appeal (against administrative actions or fines/penalties);

— security requirements;
— emergency procedures (fire, earthquake, etc);
— prohibition on sales of non-authorised products in the market;
— prohibition on the holding of any meetings in the market unless authorised by the managing authority, or prohibition of involvement in political activity in the precincts.

Practical Issues in Market Operational Management

Use of allocated space

Regular checks need to be made by managing authority staff of products being traded in the areas allocated to ensure that only authorised produce is sold, that changes have not been made to premises and that produce is not placed outside agreed boundaries. Many markets also strictly control the signs that may be painted or placed over allocated areas.

Market entry

To avoid delays at market gates most markets do not undertake other than quick inspections of incoming produce. A cargo manifest is generally obtained from the driver. Market staff generally oversee all unloading and anything not in accordance with submitted manifests is noted and reported. However, in many markets in developing countries produce enters in small vans or even on hand carts and such manifests are not available. Care must be taken in these circumstances to balance the need to obtain reliable information about quantities entering the market with the need to minimise congestion at the entrance.

Many markets now supply wholesalers, their staff, registered buyers, market staff, and loading and unloading staff with ID cards. Sometimes these can operate electronic entry gates and register entry into the market. The guiding principle for many markets in relation to vehicle entry and access is to separate vehicles delivering produce from buyers' vehicles and from vehicles taking full loads from the market.

Exclusivity for a market

In the legislation establishing many markets earlier this century governments included an exclusivity clause. These made it illegal for anyone to either operate as a wholesaler outside the market or to establish a further market without approval. This was done to safeguard the investment in the central market. In today's legal, economic and social environment of free competition, such a provision would be now difficult for governments to introduce. However, most governments have considered it necessary to have legislation or regulations concerning the establishment of wholesale markets and how wholesalers may operate. These regulations may require that no one can establish a wholesale market without prior approval and the submission of various feasibility and impact studies (e.g. regarding traffic implications).

Quality, packaging and presentation

In many more developed countries, recent decades have seen the emergence of large chain stores and supermarkets with enormous buying power. To meet their needs for large quantities and uniform qualities of a particular commodity, some producers have become specialists at supplying supermarkets. The existence of clearly defined grade standards has enabled these producers, cooperatives or their marketing agents to enter into contracts to supply large quantities, even prior to planting. Savings can be made by having appropriate selected commodities grown under controlled irrigation conditions and delivered in bulk containers directly to prepackaging plants operated by or for supermarkets.

These changes in technology and marketing practices have led to the development of larger wholesalers, larger or more integrated operations and bulk handling, with reduced handling and marketing costs per unit. Often wholesalers, who may be located in a central market, act as brokers in arranging sales of produce, but not physically handling it through the markets. Wholesale markets still have a role in helping to establish the market price, although this may become less and less relevant as long-term supply contracts are negotiated.

Under the circumstances, smaller suppliers who, in aggregate, supply a significant proportion of some commodities to a market can be disadvantaged unless care is taken to allow for their requirements in terms of unloading arrangements and other operational procedures.

All these factors can have a bearing over time on the policy adopted by the managing authority, or even government, regarding how many sections or basic trading floor units any one person or company may control. As markets change in reaction to the increasing influence of supermarkets, a policy to allow some amalgamation of trading floor units will probably be required.

Market communications

Problems arise in all big markets where changes are introduced and the various user groups do not accept or understand them. Market authorities need to devote considerable time and effort to the processes of communication and consultation with individuals and groups. Effective markets usually have the following in place:

— regular newsletters to market tenants (wholesalers and others renting space);

— a regular means of communication with representatives of other market users;

— encouragement of associations representing users, with provision for them to have offices in the market. Support to a wide range of functions for these bodies, for example, a wholesalers' association which provides business or accounting support, buyer credit arrangements, training of wholesale staff, a staff superannuation scheme and access to insurance;

— procedures to communicate what is happening in the market to the general public through media releases, publicity videos, information brochures and participation in exhibitions.

Penalties

The ultimate sanction to ensure compliance is withdrawal of the right of a wholesaler to trade in the market. This is always a serious step to take and is never easy to achieve. While withdrawal may be relatively easier when a market is new and when contracts, leases or licenses are for short periods, there can be difficulties where businesses have been established for a long period or long leases exist.

Closure of an old market

The closure of an old market and the opening of a replacement market is a complex process. The closure first has to be accepted as necessary by existing wholesalers and requires careful planning and design of the new market and the allocation of space in it. The actual shift of the location requires a concentrated and coordinated effort to minimise any loss in time for trading, to avoid traffic and other logistic problems, and to ensure that all parties are fully involved with and aware of the change.

Managing Authority

Business principles and planning

Markets do have public-service obligations. However, there are no valid reasons why a market should be required to operate at a loss for the benefit of producers, traders or consumers. For markets established and run by private enterprise there is no doubt that the objective is to make a profit. For public sector or quasi-public sector management the objectives, as a minimum, should be to ensure that all operational income and expenses are met from current income and that revenue is also sufficient to make adequate provision for long-term needs, including reserves for:

— expensive and long-term maintenance (e.g. pavement repairs; painting);

— capital replacement based on expected economic life of the buildings and equipment;

— payments for long-term loans and debts;

— long-service and retirement benefits for staff.

In some economies in transition it is argued that markets should operate on the basis of balancing operational income and expenses. This always leads to losses and problems, especially where government or municipality approval is required for fees and charges.

Administrative delays or failure to act can lead to a major discrepancy between the real cost of operation and income levels. In the United Kingdom and the United States, among others, it is the market authority that sets and approves the fee scales so these problems do not arise.

Critical staff benefits and maintenance may not be provided if income is too small. To rely on the governments or municipalities of the future to meet future capital investment costs or even to guarantee loans may not be realistic. Where governments or municipalities dictate to a managing authority that less than full cost recovery, including long-term costs, will be permitted in fee approval, then the national or local government must be prepared to subsidise the market budget.

The temptation to operate new markets on the basis of recovering only operational costs should also be avoided. From the opening day the office and computer equipment starts to depreciate, staff benefits accrue, and the buildings and pavements begin to deteriorate. Increasingly, market-managing authorities have adopted a "user-pay" principle requiring tenants, buyers, and suppliers to meet all operational and specified overhead and long-term costs.

A Business Approach

A sound business approach will include the following:

— business plan;

— annual budget;

— annual work plan;

— commercially oriented accounting system;

— monthly financial report;

— monitoring of physical performance;
— market performance and financial reports;
— monitoring and evaluation against performance indicators;
— annual financial report.

Markets should have a business plan which clearly identifies the role the market is to play and how it will do this for the benefit of the community and the market users. Long-term objectives should be included and capital replacement and new capital investment methods specified.

From this should flow an annual budget and an annual work plan on which the budget is based. There should be a commercially oriented accounting system with regular financial reports to the board of directors (at least monthly). There should also be monitoring of physical performance and ongoing monitoring and evaluation against determined performance indicators. Regular market performance and financial reports should be given to the board of directors. An annual report, with audited financial statements, should be made to government, shareholders and the public.

The accounting system

Within the overall financial structure the managing authority should ensure that it is able to identify costs and returns from the various activities in the market. As a general principle, all activities not directly related to market trading (e.g. cold stores and restaurants) should operate as separate cost centres and have separate budgets and accounts.

The accounting system, as a minimum, should enable all income and expenditure to be brought to account quickly and regularly, so as to allow regular performance reports to be prepared against budget projections. It should also:

— prevent or minimise fraudulent practices;

— allow for effective cost or expenditure control with regular income/expenditure statements;

— provide for reserves for long-term staff benefits, long-term maintenance and for capital replacement;

— show assets and liabilities;

— give a profit and loss statement.

The budget—Income and expenditure

The annual budget, approved by the board of directors prior to the commencement of the new financial year, should balance operating income and expenditure. It should also provide for long-term reserves for staff benefits, major maintenance, capital replacement and loan repayments. The budget should be based on realistic estimates of cash flow and expenditure. Most income will come from rentals or leases of market trading space and from ancillary facilities. Funds will also come from entrance and parking fees, fines and penalties, and interest earned on invested funds.

Fees can be set or based on area occupied, or on the basis of value or volumes transacted, or a combination of the two. Fees based on volumes and values are difficult to enforce and tend to encourage movement and sales of produce outside the market. *Ad-valorem* fees and tonnage-based fees do help to foster the presence of small wholesalers in the market. Such variable fees also are adjusted automatically when changes in revenue are required.

The issue of fee adjustment is usually controversial and difficult, often strongly opposed by wholesaler groups. In some markets wholesalers have threatened to withhold, or have actually withheld, payment of fees to prevent fee increases. It is important that wholesalers be consulted about fee changes and the reasons for them. Many markets have included in legislation or regulations (as against market rules prepared by the authority) a provision which puts in place automatic penalties for non-payment of fees and charges.

Many markets have, by agreement with traders' or tenants' associations, a maximum annual adjustment in fees, which is based on an independent official indicator, such as the consumer price index or cost of living index. In Spain nearly all markets apply these criteria, by agreement with market operators' organisations. Some markets have fixed rentals for a specified period of years (e.g. Nine Elms in London has a nine-year term with stipulated rentals).

Expenditure controls need rigorous application to all expenditure areas, especially high-cost areas such as staff, cleaning, maintenance, electricity, water and telephones. Staff policy and numbers must be approved by the board of directors within the annual budget. Any increases in staff numbers must be fully justified and non-performing staff should not be retained. Any increase in expenditure, or major expenditure areas above expected budget levels, must be queried by the board and investigated by management staff.

Provision in the budget must be made for a surplus above operating costs to enable transfer of funds to necessary strategic reserves. These must be carefully invested and not utilised for any purpose other than those specified.

Staff and Staff Development

Staff costs are a significant part of operational costs. It is therefore important that the board give ongoing attention, as part of budget preparation and monitoring, to staff structure including staff numbers, salary levels and training.

Staff numbers should be maintained at a level essential to fulfil the various functions of:

— management and supervision;
— accounting;
— entry control;
— entry fee collection;
— rental collection;
— unloading/loading supervision;
— produce stacking and correct use of selling floors;
— parking;
— cleaning and garbage disposal;
— maintenance (electrical, plumbing, telephones, painting);
— secretarial.

Duties and responsibilities

It is important that all staff know what their duties are, to whom they report, and what to do in the event of unusual circumstances. Every staff member should be issued with a "statement-of-duties" or "job description" which should be reviewed at least once a year by senior management.

There should be an ongoing staff-development programme funded by the annual budget. This should provide both on-the-job training and professional development, including participation by selected staff members in specific outside training. Where applicable and practicable, consideration should be given by management to provide training programmes for wholesalers, producers and buyers.

BIBLIOGRAPHY

Aaker David A., *Strategic Market Management,* Wiley, John & Sons, Incorporated, March 2007.

Abrams, Rhonda M., *The Successful Business Plan: Secrets & Strategies,* Oasis Press, 1993.

Baumbach, Clifford M. and Kenneth Lawyer, *How to Organize and Operate a Small Business.* Prentice Hall, Inc., 1989.

Coller, M., and T. L. Yohn, "Management Forecasts: What Do We Know?", *Financial Analysts Journal,* 1998.

Davis, Sid, *A Survival Guide for Selling a Home,* AMACOM/ American Management Association, 2005.

Fill, Chris, *Marketing Communications,* Hemel Hempstead: Prentice Hall, 1999.

Foster, Dennis L., *The Complete Franchise Book,* Prima Publishing and Communications, 1988.

Jeffrey Gitomer, *Real World Answers That Make Sense, Make Sales, and Make Money,* Mar 3, 2006.

Jensen, M. C., and W. H. Meckling, "Theory of the Firm: Managerial Behavior,Agency Costs, and Ownership Structure", *Journal of Financial Economics,* 1976.

Jinnett, Jerry and Linda Pinson, *Target Marketing,* Upstart Publishing Co., 1993.

John Garrison, "New Twist to Cause Marketing", *Fund Raising Management,* President National Easter Seal Society, February 1990.

Kaatz, Ron, *Advertising and Marketing Checklists,* NTC Business Books, 1993.

Ketchen, D. J., Jr., and C. L. Shook, "The Application of Cluster Analysis inStrategic Management Research: An Analysis and Critique", *Strategic ManagementJournal,* 1996.

Keup, Erwin J., *The Franchise Bible—A Comprehensive Guide,* Oasis Press/PSI Research, 1990.

Kishel, Gregory & Patricia, *Growing Your Own Business.* The Berkley Publishing Group, 1994.

Levine, John R. and Carol Barondi, *The Internet Dummies,* IDG Books, 1994.

McKeever, Mike P., *How to Write a Business Plan,* Nolo Press, 1992.

Max de Leon, "A very thin line between multilevel marketing and pyramid schemes", *The Manila Times*/April 28, 2003.

Michael J. Major, "Turning Good Deeds Into Good Business", *The International Magazine for Promotion,* February, 1992.

Moskowitz, Robert A., *The Small Business Computer Book,* Upstart Publishing Co., 1993.

Reedy, Joel, Shauna Schullo & Kenneth Zimmerman, *Electronic Marketing: Integrating Electronic Resources into the Marketing Process,* Fort Worth, TX: Dryden Press/Harcourt College, 2000.

Robert E. Linneman & John L. Stanton, *Making Niche Marketing Work: How to Grow Bigger by Acting Smaller,* 1992.

Rumbauskas, Frank, *Principles of Sales Greatness,* Sep 25, 2004.

Schiller, Dan, *Digital Capitalism: Networking the Global Marketing System,* Cambridge, MA: MIT Press, 1999.

Sitarz, Daniel, *The Complete Book of Small Business Legal Forms.* Nova Publishing, 1992.

Thomas H. Davenport and Laurence Prusak, *Working Knowledge: How Organizations Manage What They Know,* Harvard Business School Press, Boston, MA, 2000

Warner, Ralph, *Everybody's Guide to Small Claims Court,* Nolo Press, 1990.

Wallace, Patricia, *The Psychology of the Internet,* Cambridge: Cambridge University Press, 2001.

Zemke, Ron, "Winning Strategies: The 10 Commandments of Customer Service", *Incentive 169,* November 1995.

Zig Ziglar, *Selling 101: What Every Successful Sales Professional Needs to Know,* April 3, 2003.

INDEX